Worshipmania

 LOVELAND, COLORADO

Group's R.E.A.L. Guarantee to you:

Every Group resource incorporates our R.E.A.L. approach to ministry—a unique philosophy that results in long-term retention and life transformation. It's ministry that's:

This is EARL. He's R.E.A.L. mixed up. (Get it?)

 Relational
Because student-to-student interaction enhances learning and builds Christian friendships.

 Experiential
Because what students experience sticks with them up to 9 times longer than what they simply hear or read.

 Applicable
Because the aim of Christian education is to be both hearers and doers of the Word.

 Learner-based
Because students learn more and retain it longer when the process is designed according to how they learn best.

Worshipmania

Visit our Web site: **www.grouppublishing.com**

Credits
Contributors: Jay R. Ashcraft, Tim Baker, Karen Dockrey, Debbie Gowensmith, Stacy Haverstock, Trudy Hewitt, Jan Kershner, Pamela Malloy, Julie Meiklejohn, Erika Moss, Christina Schofield, Pamela J. Shoup, and Donna K. Stearns
Acquisitions Editor: Amy Simpson
Editor: Michael D. Warden
Creative Development Editor: Jim Kochenburger
Chief Creative Officer: Joani Schultz
Copy Editor: Dena Twinem
Art Director: Kari K. Monson
Cover Art Director: Jeff A. Storm
Cover Designer/Illustrator: Diana Walters
Computer Graphic Artist: Nighthawk Design and Tracy K. Donaldson
Illustrator: Amy Bryant
Production Manager: Alexander Jorgensen

Library of Congress Cataloging-in-Publication Data
Worshipmania : 80 active worship experiences for young teenagers.
    p. cm.
  Includes bibliographical references and indexes.
  ISBN 0-7644-2195-6 (alk. paper)
    1. Worship programs. 2. Church work with teenagers. I. Group Publishing.

  BV29 .W63 2000
  264'.00835--dc21

            99-088865

10 9 8 7 6 5 4 3 2   09 08 07 06 05 04 03 02 01

Printed in the United States of America.

Contents

Indexes

Introduction

Oswald Chambers once wrote:

"Worship is giving God the best that he has given you. Be careful what you do with the best you have. Whenever you get a blessing from God, give it back to him as a love gift. Take time to meditate before God and offer the blessing back to him in a deliberate act of worship" (My Utmost for His Highest).

Worship is more than a response to God's goodness or a celebration of his gifts—it is also a choice. When we choose to worship God, we deliberately humble ourselves in his presence and kneel in awe of who he is, what he has done, and what he continues to do. In all sincerity, we may believe that we recognize that God is eternal, all-knowing, all-powerful, completely holy, and full of perfect love. But until we learn the discipline of worship, we do not come to know God as we ought to know him. Worship brings us face to face with Glory. Only in worship can we say with David:

"You have made known to me the path of life;
you will fill me with joy in your presence,
with eternal pleasures at your right hand"
(Psalm 16:11).

Through worship we come to fully appreciate what God has done for us, and are overwhelmed by his marvelous character. He is the almighty God, creator of all things, ruler of the universe who descended from heaven in deliberate vulnerability. In Jesus, he gave the ultimate sacrifice for us so that we could know him and be with him without fear of judgment.

True worship means recognizing our humble standing in relationship to God, and allowing his mercy and grace to lift us to a place of honor as sons and daughters. It's from that unfathomable blessing of salvation that our song of praise springs forth. And as we worship, freely and with abandon, we are changed. We become like him.

Worshipmania is a collection of creative, unique, and inspiring worship activities for younger teenagers. These worship ideas include traditional forms of worship as well as tons of new, innovative ideas for worship. And all the ideas will help draw your students toward a deeper communion with God.

Each worship experience is based on a specific Scripture passage and theme. The ideas are versatile and easy to lead. You can use a worship idea at the beginning of a meeting on a specific Scripture passage, during a meeting on a biblical theme, or by itself in place of a regular youth meeting. You may also want to allow your students to lead the entire congregation in worship. Refer to the indexes in the back of the book (pp. 122-126) to find the worship ideas you need.

These worship experiences are designed to help you get your students excited about worship. The variety of fresh ideas will help them think and talk about what it means to worship and teach them important truths from the Bible. Most of all, these ideas will lead them to life-changing encounters with the love, majesty, and person of God.

Be Strong and Courageous!

Scripture: Joshua 23:6-8

Theme: Having Courage

Experience: In this **prayer of intercession** students will uncover ways to become more courageous for Christ.

Preparation: You'll need a Bible, a wooden dowel, a steel pipe large enough for the dowel to fit inside, and two cement blocks (you can purchase the dowel, pipe, and cement blocks at a hardware store). You'll also need a baseball bat, masking tape, markers, an instant print camera, and instant film.

Worship

Read aloud Joshua 23:6-8. Then ask:

- **What does it mean to be very strong?**
- **How is courage a form of strength?**
- **Why is strength in the form of courage important?**
- **How does it take courage to avoid following other gods?**

Say: **God goes beyond commanding Joshua to be very strong, he also tells him that there are things that will help him build his courage.**

Ask:

- **What things does God instruct Joshua to do?**
- **How can each of these things build Joshua's courage?**

Say: **I'd like you to see the difference between having courage and not having it.**

Lay the wooden dowel on the cement blocks so that the ends of the dowel are on the blocks, but the center isn't supported by them. Give students tape and markers, and have them write on the tape one thing that weakens their courage. Ideas include giving in to temptation or not trusting God. When they've written their ideas, have students tape them to the dowel. Explain to students that this wooden dowel represents us when our courage is weakened by these things. Hit the dowel with the baseball bat until it breaks.

Say: **When our courage is weakened, we're easily broken. But when we allow God to give us courage, and when we work at building it, we can stand strong.**

Hold up the steel pipe so students can see it. Give kids another piece of tape and ask them to write one thing on their tape that builds our courage. Ideas include following God, worshipping him, or reading the Bible every day. When they're finished, have students come forward and place their pieces of tape on the pipe. Take the broken dowel and slide it inside the steel pipe and lay it on the cement blocks. Explain to students that the pipe is us—when we do things that build our courage. Hit the pipe with the bat a few times. Ask:

- **When have you had this type of courage?**
- **What things in your life require you to have courage?**

Say: **This is what it looks like to have courage. With God's help, we can stand strong under any temptation, difficult situation, or pressure, and do it with confidence. His strength makes us strong.**

Have students get in groups of four and think up a situation in which most students have difficulty being courageous. For example, students might share a situation where someone needs courage to confront a friend or a sibling who's living wild. Then have groups think up a way to portray the situation in a freeze-frame picture. When groups have their ideas, have them go outside the meeting room one group at a time. As they portray their situation, take a picture of each group with the instant camera. Give each group its picture to hang on the wall. When all groups have had their pictures taken, have groups walk around and look at the pictures and guess what situation each group is portraying.

Have groups gather together in the center of the meeting room. One at a time, direct everyone's attention to each group's picture and have everyone share their guesses. Then have the group share what their situation was. Repeat this process until all groups have shared.

Say: **I'm sure that every one of us has a certain particular situation where we're struggling with having courage. I'd like you to get in groups of two, share one area of your life where you need courage, and pray for each other.**

Give students several minutes to do this. When they're finished, gather around the steel pipe and lead kids in several songs of worship—to build their courage in Christ.

A Very Special Book

Scripture: Psalm 119:97-104
Theme: Valuing God's Word

Experience: In this humorous **drama presentation** and **creative writing experience**, young people will learn about the uniqueness of the Bible and express appreciation for God's special message to them.

Preparation: You'll need Bibles, two photocopies of "A Very Special Book" script (pp. 11-12), paper, and pens or pencils. You'll also need a platter with a cover as a prop for the skit.

Worship

ive copies of the "A Very Special Book" skit (pp. 11-12) to two outgoing students and allow them to look over the script before they present it to the class. (You may want to give them the scripts several days in advance so they can practice their parts.)

Begin by asking your students:

• **Have you ever tried to put a complicated item together without using the instructions? How did it go?**

• **Have you ever had a teacher that refused to explain his or her assignments? What was that class like?**

Say: **God gave us his Word because he cares about us. He wants us to succeed at the most important assignment of all—life.**

Have students present the skit. After you have the class applaud the actors, say: **God showed his love for us by giving us this amazing book. It is his letter to us. In Psalm 119, the psalmist wrote a poem back to God showing his appreciation for God's Word.**

Read aloud Psalm 119:97-104.

Give each person a paper and a pencil or pen. Ask students to write a short letter or poem expressing their gratitude to God for giving them his Word and for how it has impacted their lives. Close by allowing volunteers to share what they have written.

Creating Worship

Scripture: Psalm 145:1-13
Theme: Praising God
Experience: In this **complete service**, students will create a worship service of praise to God.

A Very Special Book

Characters: Larry or Lorna (a typical eighth grader)

Habib (a foreign exchange student with a Middle Eastern accent)

(Habib meets Larry in the hallway at school carrying a Bible on a platter, with a cover over it.)

Larry: Habib, what have you got there?

Habib: It is a very special book!

Larry: I guess it would have to be for you to carry it around like that! Let's take a look at it. *(Habib lifts the cover.)* What, a Bible? There's nothing special about that!

Habib: I'm so sorry my friend but I am afraid you are sadly mistaken. This is a letter from the Creator of the universe to the people of the world.

Larry: *(Shaking his head)* Habib, Habib, Habib, you can't actually believe that fairy tale stuff. I mean sure, the Bible is a classic in literature, but so are works of Shakespeare, Emily Dickinson, and the Backstreet Boys.

Habib: But Larry, I know those guys put out some pretty inspiring stuff, but I never heard them claim to have words directly from God. The Bible claims over and over again to be the actual words of God.

Larry: Sure Habib, I see your point, but I could write a book and claim that it was from God, now couldn't I? No, Habib, the Bible is just another book.

Habib: Oh, no sir. I am sure you are not being right. Perhaps you could give me a list of books that, like the Bible, took sixteen hundred years to write?* A book that was written on three different continents in three different languages!*

Larry: Well, ah, ah, I ah...

Habib: Or better yet, maybe you can show me one other book that was written by more than forty different authors who came from many different walks of life.* This is true of the Bible, and yet it is unified.

Larry: Bu, bu, bu...

Habib: *(Shaking his head)* Larry, Larry, quite contrary! I wonder if you did not get your foot in front of your mouth when you said the Bible is like any other book. After all, can you name any other book written thousands of years ago that can predict tomorrow's headlines?

Larry: Well, ah...

Habib: Perhaps that cat ate your tongue my friend. Can you name another book that continues to be fresh and relevant to people's lives year after year after year?

Larry: All right Habib, give me a break.

Habib: Perhaps your brain was on a lunch break when your mouth said that the Bible is like any other book. For centuries people have been trying to attack the Bible and yet it continues to stand as the world's best selling book year after year. No Larry, it could only be the Word of God that transforms people like this book does.

Larry: *(Reaching over to put the cover back over the Bible)* Habib, you really shouldn't carry your Bible uncovered like that. I mean it's not like any other book, you know!

*From *Don't Check Your Brains at the Door* by Josh McDowell and Bob Hostetler.

Preparation: You'll need Bibles and four copies of "Our Worship Service" (p. 14).

Worship

ave students close their eyes.

Say: **Imagine for a moment that you get to stand in the presence of God for ten minutes, and then you've got to go back to Earth.**

Ask:

- **What would you say to God?**
- **What questions would you ask him?**
- **What would you do in his presence?**

Say: **For centuries, people have tried to express their awe at who God is and what he's done for them. And even though scores of people have tried, God never tires of hearing how much we love him, and how thankful we are for what he's done for us.**

Ask students to get in the following groups: "Speakers," "Singers," "Offering," and "Prayers." Give groups a copy of "Our Worship Service" (p. 14) and instruct groups to prepare their part of the service based on the handout. When they're ready, have groups follow the order of worship on the handout.

Garments of Praise

Scripture: Psalm 97

Theme: Sacrificial Praise

Experience: In this **offering** and **act of praise**, students will praise God for the things he has done in their lives.

Preparation: You'll need Bibles, extra T-shirts, and black felt-tip markers.

Worship

he week before leading this worship, ask students to bring a blank white T-shirt. Be sure to have extra blank T-shirts for students who forget their shirts.

Read aloud Psalm 97. Ask:

- **Why do you think the psalmist wrote this song?**
- **What did you notice about the psalmist's attitude toward God?**
- **What aspects of God's character does the psalmist mention?**

Our Worship Service

Singers: Prepare two songs. These can be either songs you sing, or lead the group in singing.

Speakers: Prepare two three-minute messages that help people understand how praising God affects them and God. Use Psalm 145:1-13 as a guide.

Offering: Prepare two ways people can give in response to the service. These opportunities cannot include giving money.

Prayers: Prepare two ways people can pray during the service.

The Service

- Opening Song (Singers)
- Testimony (Speakers)
- Offering (Offering)
- Song (Singers)
- Prayer (Prayers)
- Testimony (Speakers)
- Offering (Offering)
- Closing Prayer (Prayers)

Say: **The psalmist is celebrating the Lord's power and his righteous reign over all the earth. Praising God for who he is and what he's done in our lives is a natural reaction to his goodness and mercy.**

Have students form pairs and read Psalm 97 again. Ask pairs to think of one thing they would praise God for from what the psalmist mentions. For example, students might choose to praise God for his protection or his power. When they're finished, have students write their idea on the back of their T-shirts.

When they're finished, have pairs walk around the room and look at what each pair wrote on their shirts. Encourage groups to ask other groups why they chose their idea. Ask:

- **What did you notice about other people's ideas?**
- **What did you learn from listening to the psalm? Explain.**
- **How can we apply the psalmist's words to our lives?**

Say: **I'd like you to consider being people who notice God's power working in their lives, and stop to praise God for what he's done.**

Have students find a place in the room where they can be alone. Ask them to close their eyes.

Say: **Think about your life up to this point. Try to remember one moment when you experienced something miraculous that God has done in your life. Once you've got that moment in your mind, think up one word that describes it.**

Give students time to think. Then distribute markers and have students write that word on the front of their T-shirts. When they're finished, have students each find someone in the room they'd like to give their shirt to. As they give away their shirts, ask students to share their experience with the person, look them in the eyes and say, "I'd like you to experience this too." When students are finished, have them gather in the center of the classroom.

Say: **You've just offered a sacrifice of praise. You've given away something you owned, you've praised God, and you've encouraged another person to get to know God better.**

Lead students in a praise song that they know well. When you're finished, lead students in a short prayer thanking God for the things he's done in their lives.

The Service of Worship

Scripture: Matthew 25:35-40

Theme: Serving the Least

Experience: In this **service opportunity** and **sharing time**, students will look for people in their community who need to be served and serve them.

Preparation: You'll need Bibles, four city maps, and copies of the "Ways I Can Serve" handout (p. 18). Draw lines on each of the maps to separate each one into four sections: East Side, West Side, North Side and South Side. You'll also need to ask several adults to serve as drivers. Hang the following signs in different corners of the classroom: "East Side," "West Side," "North Side," and "South Side."

Worship

orm four groups. Assign each group one of the locations you've hung on the walls. Ask students to come up with a group cheer that describes the qualities of that part of the city. When they're finished, have groups present their cheers.

Say: **No matter what part of town we live in, or who we surround ourselves with, God calls us to serve people. God wants us to be people who point others to Jesus through our service.**

Have groups open their Bibles to Matthew 25:35-40 and read it together. Then ask:

• **Why does Jesus want us to know that when we serve others, we're serving him?**

• **How can we notice people who need the things that Jesus mentions in this passage?**

• **Do you think Jesus wants us to develop a lifestyle of service to others, or just serve others once in awhile? Explain.**

Say: **Jesus asks us to serve others no matter where they live or what they look like. I'd like you to spend the next few minutes living out Jesus' command.**

Distribute one city map and several "Ways I Can Serve" handouts (p. 18) to each group. Instruct groups to do as many of these types of service in the time you give them in the area of the city to which you have assigned them (East Side, South Side, etc.). However, they must perform only one service to each person. And they must try to serve as many different types of people as they can. Give groups a reasonable time limit.

When groups return, have students form new groups made up of at least one person from each of the first four groups. Have students compare experiences, sharing the highlights and things each learned from his or her experience. Ask:

• **What are some ways we can give God the glory when we do things for him that honor him?**

Have the song leader begin playing a praise song, and ask kids to join in worshipping God together. When the song ends, ask a few groups to share some of the things they learned and felt from this activity. Afterward, have the song leader begin playing another song. Repeat this process until every group has shared.

Gather groups together to form one large group. Ask volunteers to share one awesome thing they heard another person share in their smaller groups. After students have shared, close the worship time with a short praise song and a prayer.

The Reckless Raging Fury

Scripture: Ephesians 3:16-21

Theme: God's Love

Experience: In this **prayer of thanksgiving** and **creative writing experience**, students will explore God's love.

Preparation: You'll need Bibles, one blanket for every two students, index cards, duct tape (or other tape with strong adhesive bond), newsprint, and pens.

Worship

ave students form two groups and sit in circles. Distribute index cards, markers, and tape to both groups. Have one group think up descriptive words for God's love. Ideas include "unconditional" and "powerful." Give blankets to this group and instruct them to tape their ideas to one side of their blankets. Have the second group think up difficult moments in their lives. Ideas include getting a bad grade on a test or fighting with a sibling. Instruct this group to tape their ideas to each other.

Ways I Can Serve

- Hold open doors

- Give out spare change

- Carry shopping bags to cars

- Sweep sidewalks

- Buy someone a soda

- Help gather shopping carts

- Wash windshields

- Pick up trash

- Rake a yard

- Give away free hugs

- Feed parking meters (put coins in meters that are about to run out)

Say: **Let's spend some time getting a hands-on idea of what God's love is really like.**

Have groups go to opposite ends of the room. Explain that the group without blankets must walk from one side of the room to the other, while the blanket group tries to catch them with their blankets (index cards facing out). When a walker is caught, the blanket group must wrap him or her up tight, hold for ten seconds, then set him or her free. Walkers may try to resist the blanket people but are not allowed to run.

Give students the signal to begin. Remind students to be careful not to hurt others while playing this game. Be sure to play the game several times, and allow groups to switch roles if they want. When groups switch roles, have the walkers place their index cards on the new group of walkers.

After the game, ask:

• **What did you learn about God's love from this activity?**

• **When have you felt that God's love comforted you when you were hurting? Explain.**

• **Why do we sometimes resist the love and comfort of God (and others) when we are hurting?**

Say: **God's word gives us an awesome picture of what his love is like. I'd like you to read it.**

Have volunteers read aloud Ephesians 3:16-21. Then ask:

• **How does it feel knowing that God's love is so big? Explain.**

• **What might cause you to doubt that God's "big" love always surrounds you?**

• **What are some ways we can access God's love and comfort when we are hurting?**

Say: **I'd like you to consider for a moment how awesome it is that God would love us. He doesn't have to love us; he wants to. And even when we make a big mistake, he longs to wrap us in his love and comfort us.**

Ask the original two groups to each write a prayer of thanksgiving for God's love on a sheet of newsprint. When they're finished, have both groups cover themselves with the blankets, and read their prayers aloud. Close with a short prayer thanking God for his love.

Serving God While You're Young

Scripture: 1 Timothy 4:12

Theme: Serving God Now

Experience: In this **prayer of petition** and **creative reading**, teenagers will compare typical adult attitudes with God's attitude toward young people.

Preparation: You'll need a Bible. You'll also need to write the closing prayer on a white board or on poster board.

Worship

Tell students they're about to participate in a survey about typical adult attitudes toward young teens. Have your students all gather in the middle of the room.

Then say: **After each question I ask, you'll have three choices, "a," "b" or "c." If you choose "a," move to the left side of the room. If you choose "b," stay in the middle of the room. If you think "c" is the most accurate answer, move to the right side of the room.**

Read the following questions, allowing your young people to move to the appropriate place after each question is asked. (You may want to stop and ask various participants why they chose the answers they did after each survey question.)

1. **Most adults think middle school/high school students are**
   a) **immature,**
   b) **reasonably mature, or**
   c) **more mature than they were as teenagers.**

2. **When teenagers enter a store, they are**
   a) **more likely to be suspected of shoplifting,**
   b) **less likely to be suspected of shoplifting, or**
   c) **more likely to catch a shoplifter than to be one.**

3. **Most young people are likely to be**
   a) **irresponsible,**
   b) **responsible, or**
   c) **halfway responsible half the time.**

4. Most adults

    a) don't have a clue about the pressures young people face,

    b) understand the pressure young people face, or

    c) kind of understand where kids are coming from.

Read 1 Timothy 4:12. In pairs allow young people to discuss any differences between God's attitude toward young people and the typical adult's attitude toward young people. After you have reassembled the group, allow your students to share some of their answers.

Ask your students to pause for a few minutes and silently ask God how he might want to use them for his service this year. Encourage them to think big as they picture what God may want them to do. Ask for volunteers to share their ideas on how God might use them.

Ask your young people to consider the following prayer as you read it from the board: **Lord, may we never give adults an excuse to look down on us because of our age. Instead, may we be an example by using our words, life, love, faith, and purity in your service. In the name of Jesus, amen.**

Close by asking your students to pray this personalized prayer (from 1 Timothy 4:12) together, then ask kids to take turns worshipping God by thanking him for specific ways his power and grace has influenced their lives.

How We Give

Scripture: 2 Corinthians 9:6-7

Theme: Giving

Experience: In this **creative reading** and **act of commitment**, students will commit to give generously.

Preparation: You'll need Bibles, and one copy of the "Who Gets It?" handout (p. 23) for each student.

Worship

Say: **Let's get started with a quick quiz. I'd like you to find a place alone and answer questions about that all-important subject—your money. When you're finished, get together with another person and discuss your responses.**

Give each student a copy of "Who Gets It?" (p. 23). When students are finished, help them get in pairs with another person and share their answers.

Gather everyone together and ask:

- **Who gave away all of the money? Why?**
- **Who gave away all but five dollars? Why?**
- **Who kept most of the money? Why?**
- **Who did you give the most money to? Why?**

Say: **God wants us to see people in need, and trust him enough to give them whatever he leads us to give.**

Read 2 Corinthians 9:6-7. Then ask:

- **What does it mean to sow sparingly?**
- **What does it mean to sow generously?**
- **Why is giving cheerfully so important to God?**

Say: **How we give is just as important as what we give. God doesn't want us to be unaware of the needs around us, and he doesn't want us to know about the needs others have and then ignore them. I'd like us to commit to being people who are aware of others' needs, and people who give to those needs generously. I'd like you to join me in this responsive reading.**

Have students gather in a circle and read the following commitment together. After reading each sentence, have everyone repeat it.

Father God, we ask that you make us aware of the needs of others around us. Some people we know are physically hurt or sick. Make us people who can offer physical healing. Some people we know are angry, depressed, or grieving. Make us people who can offer emotional wholeness. Some people we know are hungry and need food. Make us people who will give what we have to fill them. Lord we ask that you change us. Cause us to seek out the needs of others with eager hearts. Push us into the lives of others so that we can offer them what they really need—you. Amen.

When you've finished the reading, close the meeting by having group members give one another hugs.

Who Gets It?

You only have ten dollars in your pocket. Read through these situations and decide who (if anyone) will get your money and how much of it they'll get. Be sure not to go over your ten dollars.

- You're at the mall with some friends. A young lady walks up to you holding a small baby. She asks you for ten dollars to buy the baby some formula.

- You're out for a walk one afternoon. You pass a nicely dressed man who's lying on the sidewalk bleeding. He's mumbling, "Please, help me. They took all my money. I need thirty-five cents to call my wife."

- A man who is drunk approaches you one afternoon after school. He reeks of alcohol. In slurred speech, he tells you that his car has broken down. He needs ten dollars—bus fare to get to the next town.

- A nicely dressed woman driving a very nice car stops at a stop sign and waves you over. "Please, can you help me?" she asks. "I'm late for a meeting, and I don't have any money for the toll booth ahead. I'll repay you, and give you a small reward if you would just loan me five dollars."

- Your youth pastor asks the youth group to consider sponsoring a child in a Third World country. He shows you an emotionally compelling video then begins passing his ball cap around the group.

Confessions of a Teenage Christian

Scripture: James 5:16

Theme: Confessing Sin

Experience: In this **sharing time** and **prayer of confession**, students will talk about the times they've sinned and ask forgiveness.

Preparation: You'll need a Bible, markers, paper, pencils, and newsprint. Hang sheets of newsprint with the following headings on the wall of your meeting room: "Things I've Done," "Things I've Said," and "Things I've Thought."

Worship

ave students get in groups of three. Say: **I'd like you to think of one famous person you really admire. It can be a rock star, athlete, writer, speaker, or anyone you want. I'd like you to come up with a quick mime that will give us clues as to who this person is.**

Give groups several minutes. When they're finished, have groups present their people. Then ask:

• **How much time do you think these people spend trying to be the best at what they do?**

• **When you're this famous, do you think it's important to think about what you do all the time? Why?**

• **Would these people be good at what they do if they chose to practice only one day a week? Explain.**

Say: **I'd like you to hear something from the Bible about how we're supposed to live the Christian life.**

Read James 5:16. Ask:

• **What does it mean to confess our sins so we can be healed?**

• **How does keeping our sins secret affect us?**

• **Why is it important to be honest with God and each other when we mess-up? Explain.**

Ask students to look at the sheets of newsprint hanging on the wall.

Say: **I'd like you to think of times that you haven't lived up to God's** expectations. I'd like you to take a marker and go to these sheets and write times you've messed up in these areas.

Allow students time to write on the newsprint. When they're finished, take the sheets of newsprint off the wall and lay them face up on the floor. Have students make a circle around them. Ask:

- **How do these mess-up's we've listed impact our relationship with God?**
- **How do these impact our relationships with one another?**

Distribute paper and pencils to students. Ask students to work individually to write a prayer to God asking him to forgive them for times when they've messed up and not lived like they should.

Say: **The cool thing is that when we blow it, God's forgiveness erases our mistake and we can live like we're brand-new.**

Have students close by silently praying the prayers each wrote, then asking God to help him or her live for him.

Giving Everything to Jesus

Scripture: Philippians 3:7-11

Theme: Sacrificing for Jesus

Experience: In this **offering** and **celebration of the Lord's Supper**, students will commit to living for Jesus rather than possessions.

Preparation: You'll need a Bible, one balloon for each student, felt-tip markers, a pin, a cassette or CD player, and instrumental music. You'll also need to invite someone authorized by your church to serve the Lord's Supper to your students.

Worship

ive each student a balloon. Say: **I know a guy who can get you a job in a circus. In fact, he's looking for people who can do unbelievable feats with balloons. So, find someone to pair up with and come up with an astounding balloon feat that will amaze us all.**

Have students form pairs and create their balloon feats. When they're finished, have them perform their balloon stunts. As they're performing, instruct the audience to ooh and aah at their stunts. Ask:

- **When have you had to "juggle" your desire to buy something you** really wanted because you didn't have enough money?

• Is it OK to strongly desire a new shirt, video game, or other material possession? Explain.

• What's wrong with wanting to have more possessions?

• Is it OK to desire these things more than we desire God? Explain.

Say: **Having things is neat, but when the desire for these things becomes more than our desire to be like Christ, then we're living out of focus. The Apostle Paul helps us understand how we should view the things we have.**

Read Philippians 3:7-11. Then ask:

• What does it mean to consider the things we have as unimportant? Explain.

• Why does Paul stress knowing Jesus over having possessions?

Say: **Knowing and serving Jesus is more important than having the newest gadget or any other material possession. I'd like you to think about any possession you have that sometimes seems more important to you than Jesus. It could be your clothes, your stereo, your car, even your telephone.**

Play some quiet worship music and ask students to think and pray quietly. Ask students to think of one possession they'd like to sacrifice as an act of devotion to Christ. For example, kids might choose to give away some clothes or take a "fast" from talking on the telephone. Distribute markers and have students write that possession on their balloon.

Say: **Let's sacrifice these things and commit to focusing on Jesus.**

Begin playing some soft worship music. Ask your authorized leader to begin calling students forward to receive the Lord's Supper. As students come forward, ask them to leave their balloons at the altar. When everyone has received the Lord's Supper, say: **Jesus, we give you these things.**

Begin using the pin to pop the balloons. When you're finished, gather the popped balloons into a pile and have students gather around them. Ask students to pray and ask God to help them keep their commitments.

Let Peace Rule

Scripture: John 14:27; Colossians 3:15-17
Theme: Peace in Jesus

Experience: In this **meditation** and **sharing time**, students will discuss what having peace means.

Preparation: You'll need a Bible.

Worship

ave students get in groups of four. Say: **You've been contracted by the National Institute of Monkey Research to help with a research project. They're convinced that they can increase the intelligence of monkeys if they're raised in the right environment. The Institute would like you to explore some different environments and see what effect they might have on the intellectual development of monkeys. I'd like two people in your group to pretend they're monkeys. Create a way to respond to your researchers' attempts. I'd like the other two people in your group to pretend you're researchers. I'd like you to do whatever you can to create the environment that I assign you.**

Assign researchers one of the following growth environments: peace, hostility, chaos, indifference, touch. Feel free to create your own environment ideas, but be sure to assign at least one group the peace environment.

When groups are ready, have them present their research. Then ask:

- **Which of these environments would really work?**
- **Which of these environments would work with you?**
- **Is peace an important environment to be in? Why?**
- **How can we create peace in our lives?**

Say: **The Apostle Paul knew about peace. And even though his life was filled with times when there was no peace, he was still able to find it.**

Read Colossians 3:15-17. Have students get back in their groups and discuss the following questions:

- **How can we let the peace of Christ rule in our hearts? Explain.**
- **How does God's Word dwelling in us create peace in our lives?**
- **How does peace direct the way we live?**

Have students find a place where they can get comfortable and close their eyes. Tell students that you're going to read two statements and you'd like them to think about the statements.

- **Think about a place that you consider to be perfectly peaceful.**

• **Imagine you're resting in the lap of Jesus. Describe the peace that you feel.**

Have students sit in a circle. Read John 14:27.

Say: **God gives us peace. Isn't that powerful? No matter what the world throws at us, we can find peace if we'll turn to God. We've all experienced God's peace at one time or another. Let's talk about a time when you felt God's peace.**

Ask students to think of a time when they knew God was giving them peace. Then have students go around the circle and share the time when God gave them peace. Students might begin by saying something like, "God gave me peace when..."

Then say: **Imagine that you're talking to God and asking him to help you have more peace in your life. What do you think he might say?**

After you've given students time to think through the last statement, instruct them to whisper prayers to God, asking him for more peace in their lives. Close by whispering your own prayer for peace in the lives of your students.

Loving Others Well

Scripture: 1 John 4:7-8, 19-21

Theme: Loving Others

Experience: In this **drama presentation, act of commitment,** and **offering,** students will discover how they can love others in the group and beyond.

Preparation: You'll need Bibles, craft paper, staplers, tape, markers, and a copy of "Loving Others?" (p. 30). Before the worship, copy the handout and cut apart the situations.

Worship

When students have arrived, have them get in three groups. Give each group one situation from the "Loving Others?" handout (p. 30). Explain to groups that you'd like them to act out what's on the paper. Then, you'd like them to create whatever ending they'd like—either one where the people act lovingly toward each other, or one where they act without love. If you have more students than characters, have some students act as props in the skit, or have them create new characters for the skit. When groups are ready, have them present their skits.

After the skits, ask:

- **When have you encountered situations like these? Tell us about it.**
- **How would you have handled these situations?**
- **What effect does unconditional love have on difficult situations?**

Have students form pairs and read 1 John 4:7-8, 19-21.

Say: **If loving each other is the way we reflect God's love in our lives, then we've got to work hard at loving each other regardless of how we feel or what other people do to us. I'd like us to try an experiment. Let's commit to loving each other for the next seven days. When we come back next week, we'll talk a bit more about how we did.**

Give pairs paper, staplers, tape, and markers. Have pairs create a three-dimensional symbol that represents their commitment to love others for the next week. For example, groups might want to make a three dimensional heart with the words "Love my enemies" or several hands in a circle and write "Love everyone I meet."

When groups are finished, ask them to bring their creations and follow you to the sanctuary.

Say: **I'd like to challenge you to really love your friends. We can't say we love God and then not love people. Love is the way people will know that we belong to God.**

Ask groups to come forward and place their symbol on the altar of your church. As they're laying their creations on the altar, have one in the pair share what their creation represents. Then have the other person in the pair share a sentence prayer asking God to help them keep their commitment to love others.

When groups have placed their creations, say: **Congratulations on the commitment you've made. Now, for the next seven days, I'd like you to keep in contact with the other person in your pair. Tell each other how you're doing with your commitment, and encourage each other.**

Close the worship by praying for your students and asking God to help them with their commitments for the next seven days.

At your next meeting, have pairs talk about how they did with their commitments, what types of struggles they encountered, and what God taught them through the week.

Loving Others?

Jesse has been angry for a long time. He's been woke up every night this week by his parents screaming at each other. He walked in to youth group tonight angry. When William tried to high five him, Jesse shoved him and ran out.

Teresa told her friend Sarah that she is pregnant from Mac, her boyfriend of three months. Sarah is telling everyone. She leans over and tells you about it and then says, "That's it for me. I'm NEVER talking to her again."

You've been friends with Larry for three years. You love having him as a friend, but you don't trust him much. He's always telling you about his lawn-mowing business, and how he tells his customers that he mows their lawn while they're at work, but often doesn't. And he continues to collect the money. Your parents asked Larry to mow the lawn every week this summer.

Pictures of God

Scripture: Mark 12:28-30

Theme: God's Uniqueness

Experience: In this **artistic experience** and **meditation**, teenagers will put the words of the Bible passage into rebus form.

Preparation: You'll need paper, markers, and extra Bibles. Before class lay paper along the edges of the room with a marker or two beside each page, enough for the teenagers you expect. Have spare paper handy.

Worship

Make certain every person has a Bible. Read Mark 12:28-30. Then say: **We will worship God today by focusing on each word of this passage. This passage tells us not only a reason to worship God but a way to worship him. To worship word by word, change at least every other word into a simple picture. For example "hear" can become an ear, and "strength" can be represented by a strong arm. As you draw, meditate on the reasons God is uniquely wonderful.**

Explain that when you say "go," youth will race to the paper of their choice and begin drawing. Then say: **Go!** Have kids hurry to the paper on the edge of the room and start drawing the passage. Walk around to make certain each person finds Mark 12:28-30 in his or her Bible.

On your second trip around the room, affirm a specific drawing for each person. Let the ideas be paramount, but don't neglect to affirm good artistic work. Thank and affirm everyone for worshipping God so well through illustrations.

Here's a sample rebus of one phrase in verse 29 of the passage:

When kids have finished their rebuses, have them move three rebuses to the left and solve that rebus (without looking at their Bibles), then three more to the left and solve that rebus. The different pictures will help each youth memorize Mark 12:28-30.

Call the group's attention to you and read the passage in unison with youth speaking from memory. Ask:

• **How have you shown love to God in one of these ways?**

Close with prayer, having group members take turns praising God in sentence prayers for his unique qualities and for giving us the ability to worship him in so many creative ways.

Choose Life!

Scripture: Deuteronomy 30:19-20

Theme: Choosing Life

Experience: In this **declaration of faith** and **artistic experience**, youth will create credit cards as a testimony to their willingness to bank on choosing life.

Preparation: You'll need poster board, chalkboard, chalk, and ballpoint pens. Before the experience cut the poster board into credit card–sized rectangles.

Worship

old up a credit card. Ask:

• **What is this good for?**

• **Where can I spend it?**

• **Why am I the only one authorized to spend it?**

Use your students' responses to transition into focus on Deuteronomy 30:19-20. Read the passage, then say: **There is credit that is even more powerful than money. It is "choice." You are credited with a certain number of choices and you get to decide how to use them in this life.**

Ask:

• **What does Deuteronomy 30:19-20 have to say about this?**

• **Why are you the only one who can spend your choices?**

• **What is a specific example of how you have chosen life and blessings?**

• **Even when we don't mean to choose death and curses, certain behaviors lead to those. What's an example of a behavior that leads to death and curses?**

Write Deuteronomy 30:19-20 on the chalkboard. Then have kids fill the chalkboard with illustrations of life-producing choices and death-producing choices. Then pass out the poster board rectangles and direct students to each make a credit card that expresses his or her commitment to choose life and blessings in Christ. Suggest that kids pattern it after a credit card and Deuteronomy 30:19-20. Include features like:

- logo,
- motto,
- instructions for activating the spending power of the card,
- expiration date, and
- fine-print instructions.

Circulate and encourage kids to focus on God as they make the cards.

Call for volunteers to read their cards as a way to proclaim their faith as an act of worship. Suggest they keep these in their wallets or billfolds as reminders to choose life.

Breaking the Power of Shame

Scripture: Psalm 32:1-5

Theme: Overcoming Shame

Experience: In this **drama presentation** and **prayer of confession,** youth will overcome shame.

Preparation: You'll need extra Bibles, chalkboard, chalk, index cards, pens or pencils, and a large room.

Worship

ll youth hold in secret sins that they don't want anyone to know about. They're ashamed, fearful they'll get caught, or worried that someone won't like them anymore if these sins become known. They don't always need to confess these wrongdoings to a person, but they always need to confess to God. This worship service leads youth to do this.

When all the students have arrived, gather the group in the middle of the room with their Bibles, and invite them to share their ideas for dramatizing Psalm 32:1-5. On a chalkboard, jot down their ideas as students state them, putting beside each idea the initials of the one who suggests it. As the group chooses how to dramatize the passage, suggest they use mime and insist they use at least one idea from each person.

Here's a sample drama to pick and choose from:

Blessed is he—Youth hold up their hands happily to represent turning to God.

Whose transgressions—Youth use their arms to form an "X" over their faces.

Are forgiven, whose sins are covered—Youth give each other hugs of forgiveness, or bow before God.

Blessed is the man whose sin the Lord does not count against him—One youth walks around and appears to make a sin tally, then throws away the list.

And in whose spirit is no deceit—Youth look at each other with honesty.

When I kept silent—All youth put hands over their own mouths as though hiding something.

My bones wasted away—Youth look very weak and tired.

Through my groaning all day long—Youth silently wail and moan.

For day and night—Youth make arcs like sun rising and then moon rising.

Your hand was heavy upon me—Youth in pairs or trios, one being weighed down by the hand of the other.

My strength was sapped as in the heat of summer—Youth fan themselves and look weak.

Then I acknowledged my sin to you and did not cover up my iniquity—Youth take out "sins" and show God, like taking cards out of pocket and showing upward to let God "read" them.

I said "I will confess my transgressions to the Lord"—Youth bow on knee to God.

And you forgave the guilt of my sin—Youth look up with obvious relief.

When they're ready, have kids present the mime one or two times. Then give each person an index card and a pen or pencil. For the next few minutes, invite kids to write on their cards any "hidden sin" that they feel ashamed of. Collect the cards, and read each one silently. One by one, take each card, tear it up and throw it on the floor, and have kids say in unison: **Jesus forgives you!** Encourage kids to confess their sins to someone they trust, and pray with that person, seeking God's forgiveness, and asking God to break the power of shame in their lives.

God Really Cares!

Scripture: Psalm 32:6-11
Theme: Hearing God
Experience: In this **sharing time**, and **creative writing experience**

youth will invite God's advice and write what they sense him saying.

Preparation: You'll need extra Bibles, paper, and pencils.

Worship

Read Psalm 32:6-11. Point out that God says in Psalm 32:8, "I will instruct you and teach you in the way you should go." Invite kids to share up to three words that describe their response to the fact that the God of the universe cares about their problems and their joys. Let no one use the same words any other person uses.

Then say: **Let's ask God for his advice on a particular situation you're facing. It could be a very happy situation, or a very sad situation, or one in which you just aren't certain what to do next. I'll give you paper and you write the situation.**

After kids have written the situation, say: **Now search Psalm 32:6-11 for hints of what to do. Write down the phrase that God most wants you to apply to your situation.**

After youth write their phrases, take them one step further. Say: **Now, based on what you discovered in the passage, listen to God for a bit. What is he telling you to do? What actions does he want you to take? What attitudes does he want you to express? What does he want you to stop? What does he want you to continue? What does he want you to start? Record his answers on your paper as you sense them.**

Write these questions on poster board or a chalkboard to guide students' listening and writing:

- What actions does he want you to take?
- What attitudes does he want you to express?
- What does he want you to stop?
- What does he want you to continue?
- What does he want you to start?

Invite volunteers to read a single sentence that they believe God is telling them, insisting that no one reveal personal information. Assure kids that God does communicate with us, and though it can be very hard to know what he's saying, we can keep listening until we understand.

Invite kids to privately pray one more time, listening to God rather than speaking, and jotting down what they understand God saying to them. Then have kids take turns praying aloud, praising God for caring about the problems in our lives.

Together We Stand

Scripture: Ecclesiastes 4:9-12
Theme: Friendship
Experience: In this **creative movement**, students will demonstrate the strength of friendship.
Preparation: You'll need a Bible and enough strips of yarn so that each person can give one strip to every other person in the group.

Worship

Read Ecclesiastes 4:9-12. Have students form pairs. If possible, have kids create same-sex pairs to increase comfort for this creative movement. Direct the pairs to move as far apart as your room allows. Then direct them to perform the actions below as a pair, first slowly in a practice run with many stops for clarification, and then more quickly until pairs can do the whole thing without interruption. For the final run through, have leaders read the Scripture as students act it out. Let this final run through be an offering to God.

Two are better than one because they have a good return for their work—Everyone spreads and then pairs come together and smile.

If one falls down, his friend can help him up—One falls and then the partner helps him or her up. Then the other falls and the partner helps him or her up.

But pity the man who falls and has no one to help him up!—Each member falls individually and looks around but no one is there.

Also, if two lie down together, they will keep warm—Partners lie on the floor back to back.

But how can one keep warm alone?—Partners separate and lie alone, shivering.

Though one may be overpowered, two can defend themselves—Partners stand back to back and both hold up their fists in a defensive pose.

A cord of three strands is not quickly broken—Three people of neighboring pairs stand while the fourth tries unsuccessfully to knock them down. Trade roles three times.

Call pairs back together and invite them to speak aloud to God the phrase they appreciate most in this passage. Then ask each person to tell God a different reason he or she appreciates the gift of friendship. Give each person several strips of yarn as a reminder that they have not just one friend but a whole group of friends in this church. Urge them to show friendship to each other by giving one strip of yarn to each person in the group.

The Word Made Flesh

Scripture: John 1:1-5

Theme: Christmas

Experience: In this seasonal **prayer of thanksgiving**, teenagers will thank God for coming to Earth as a baby.

Preparation: You'll need extra Bibles and poster board or a chalkboard. Before the experience, write the prayer starters on the board.

Worship

John 1:1-5 is the forgotten Christmas story. Use it during the Christmas season to avoid "We study this every year!" Start by emphasizing that the Almighty God came to earth as a human baby and grew here so we could know what he is like. This ultimate love action is hard to put into words, but John 1:1-5 does a great job of it.

Guide youth in a unique prayer of thanksgiving for this love action of God— in which the prayer spells out "Christmas." For each "prayer starter" listed below, have one or more of your kids quote or paraphrase a portion of John 1:1-5, and complete the statement that follows. Continue until kids have spelled out "Christmas" and completed this unique prayer of thanks.

Christ was at creation. I like this about you, God, because…

He brings life. I see this life…

Really, God, you became human so we could know you. I find this awesome because…

In the beginning was the Word. I find it amazing that…

Shine in the darkness, you do. I see this…

Through you everything was made. Thanks for making…

My life is ___ because…

A light in my life you are. This year I've noticed this when…

Show me…

Let the prayer lead to discussing these mysteries. Ask:

• **What amazes you most about Jesus' birth?**

• **How does it make you feel to know that the God of the universe allowed himself to become a human baby because he wanted to reach you?**

• **What are some things about Christmas for which you would most like to thank God? Explain.**

Meditations on Love

Scripture: Romans 8:37-39

Theme: God's Love

Experience: During this **creative reading** and **meditation**, kids will bask in the truth that they are secure because God will never leave them.

Preparation: You'll need extra Bibles, all in the NIV translation.

Worship

Young teens have a lot to fear—violence at school or home, friends who choose to abandon them, illness and injury, changes of all kinds. But there's one truth that gets them through all this—God and his unchanging love for them.

Guide kids to read Romans 8:37-39 in three ways, each time filling in the words you leave out. You'll need to be sure all youth have the NIV Bible translation. As they fill in words, they'll memorize how secure they are in God.

Reading 1: Read it first with these words left out (*the words to be filled in are in italics*). This reading focuses on all the things that threaten to separate kids from God: "**No, in all __ __**(*these things*) **we are more than conquerors through him who loved us. For I am convinced that neither __**(*death*) **nor __** (*life*), **neither __** (*angels*) **nor __** (*demons*), **neither the __** (*present*) **nor the __** (*future*), **nor any __** (*powers*), **neither __** (*height*) **nor __** (*depth*), **nor __ __** (*anything else*) **in all creation, will be able to separate us from the love of God that is in Christ Jesus our Lord.**"

Reading 2: This reading focuses on the reasons why we can't be separated from God (*the missing words are in italics*): "**No, in all these things __ __ __ __ __** (*we are more than conquerors*) **through __ __ __ __**(*him who loved us*). **For __ __ __** (*I am convinced*) **that __** (*neither*) **death nor life, __** (*neither*) **angels nor demons, __** (*neither*) **the present __** (*nor*) **the future, __** (*nor*) **any powers, __** *(neither)* **height nor depth,** __ *(nor)* **anything else in all creation, will be able to separate us from the** __ __ __ *(love of God)* **that is in** __ __ __ __ *(Christ Jesus our Lord)."*

Reading 3: Gather youth in trios. If your group has six or fewer, stay in one group. Have kids take turns reading a phrase and leaving out a word, the word they most want to emphasize. The complete passage is: **"No, in all these things we are more than conquerors through him who loved us. For I am convinced that neither death nor life, neither angels nor demons, neither the present nor the future, nor any powers, neither height nor depth, nor anything else in all creation, will be able to separate us from the love of God that is in Christ Jesus our Lord."**

Now challenge volunteers to recite as much of the passage as they can remember as a thank you prayer to God. Invite each youth to thank God for a specific fear God gets him or her through. Finally, say in unison: **Thank you, God, for staying with us always.**

Show No Favorites

Scripture: James 2:1-13

Theme: Favoritism

Experience: During this **creative writing experience** and **meditation,**
kids will discover how to live James 2:1-13 in their own lives.

Preparation: You'll need extra Bibles, paper, and pens or pencils.

Worship

avoritism has become something Christians do and think nothing of. Especially in the middle school years, Christian kids say all the right answers during Bible study and then walk into the hall and cruelly put down a young person they consider less important than they are. Young teens seldom mean to hurt people, but the damage is just as real and just as lasting.

To overcome this destructive pattern, guide kids to treat other people the way they would treat Jesus if he were in their school.

To begin, form three groups and have kids in each group rewrite James 2:1-13 in their own words based on one of these settings:

• anywhere the popular or unpopular labels are used (example for verses 2-4:

"Suppose a student comes into your meeting wearing the latest fashion and another comes in wearing clothes that are out of style. If you show special attention to the popular student wearing fine clothes by talking freely to him and giving one-word answers to the other guy, you are shallow and have become a judge with evil thoughts.");

• in the lunchroom at your school;

• in a setting where people from two cliques come together, such as a school classroom or sporting event.

As groups write their paraphrases, remind them to let the Scripture speak to them. Have them invite God to show them mistakes they make in the way they treat people.

When groups are ready, have them take turns reading their paraphrases. Then discuss these questions:

• **When you wrote your paraphrase, what phrases in James 2:1-13 convicted you of a change you need to make in the way you treat people?** (Invite each to share a specific, but do not allow names or identifying details.)

• **How can you treat each person just like you would treat Jesus?**

• **How can treating others with equal respect become a way to worship God every day?**

• **Why do people show favoritism? Why do you?**

• **What can you do this week to obey God's Word in James 2:1-13?**

Love Is Worship

Scripture: 1 John 4:18
Theme: Loving Others
Experience: In this **sharing time** and **commissioning**, teenagers will be sent out in confidence rather than in fear.
Preparation: You'll need extra Bibles, and a pair of magnets for each person.

Worship

ive each person a pair of magnets and instruct kids to set the poles so they repel (north will repel north; south will repel south; but north and south will attract). Let them have fun chasing the one magnet around the floor with the repelling pole. Then challenge kids to find the two repelling forces in 1 John 4:18. They are love and fear.

Say: **Each time we show real love to someone, we worship God. Because we believe in Jesus, we're eager to worship God in everyday life. So let's commit to do this! We can repel our fears and love in God's name instead!**

Have kids hold up one magnet and call out a fear that keeps them from loving. Then have kids hold up the other magnet and "repel" the fear by calling out a way they can show love in spite of that fear.

If kids have trouble coming up with fears and ways to overcome them, suggest they skim 1 John 4:1-21 for ideas. Here are some examples:

• I'll repel the fear of shyness by going ahead and acting friendly even though I'm scared, remembering that "perfect love drives out fear" (4:18).

• I'll repel the fear that people might think I'm weak by remembering that "God is love," and God is the most powerful force there is (4:8).

• I'll repel the fear that I'll look stupid by remembering that God gave up power to come live here and "since God so loved us, we also ought to love one another" (4:11).

After kids voice their fears and tell ways they can overcome them, form groups of four or fewer and have kids tell each of their partners one thing they love about each other as a brother or sister in Christ. For example, kids might say "I love your laugh," or "I love the way you accept everyone." When kids are finished, remind the group that loving others is one of the most important ways we honor God and worship him.

Let kids keep the magnet sets as reminders to repel fear with love, and to let God's love control them rather than fear control them.

That Future Deliverance

Scripture: Revelation 21:1-4

Theme: Hope

Experience: In this **act of praise** and **prayer of thanksgiving**, young people will anticipate that joyful time when sorrow and pain will be done away with.

Preparation: You'll need a Bible, markers, and newsprint. Before the experience lay a long sheet of newsprint along the floor.

Worship

As kids enter, give them markers and direct them to a position along the newsprint on the floor. Challenge them to fill the newsprint with drawings or descriptions of everything that makes them sad. Ideas might include:

- my grandfather dying,
- not being able to see,
- other disabilities,
- ugliness between friends and enemies,
- abused children,
- broken families,
- drunk drivers who kill innocent people, or
- cancer.

After several minutes, ask kids to take turns explaining their drawings. Then say: **There is a lot to be sad about in the world today. But God has promised that it won't always be this way.**

Ask a volunteer to read Revelation 21:1-4 as a celebration that the Giver of all good things will make certain that things won't always be sad and bad. Invite each person to tell why this passage gives him or her power to make it through the present struggles of life. Direct kids to spend time together in prayer, thanking God and offering him praise for the promise of deliverance from sorrow and suffering.

After the prayer, invite kids to share other Bible promises that give them hope and help during sad and bad times. Encourage kids to direct these as offerings of praise to God.

In closing, invite kids to name ways they can help each other through the hard times and shine God's light in the world's darkness. Insist that these be actions rather than just words.

Close the worship time by singing a song about heaven or God's power to help us through tough times.

Putting On the Law

Scripture: Deuteronomy 6:4-9

Theme: Obeying God

Experience: In this **artistic experience** and **act of praise**, teenagers will create symbols to remind themselves to follow God, then paint the symbols on each other's faces.

Preparation: You'll need a Bible, paper, pencils, and face paint (available at many department stores, party-supply stores, and toy stores).

Worship

Read aloud Deuteronomy 6:4-9. Have students form pairs to discuss these questions:

> • **How can we show that we love God with all our heart, soul, and strength?**

> • **Why did Moses instruct the Israelites to tie God's commands as symbols on their hands, bind them on their foreheads, and so on?**

> • **How can we remember to love God and follow his commands today?**

Distribute paper and pencils, and have pairs brainstorm simple symbols that could remind them to love God and follow God's commands—an arrow pointing toward heaven or a heart with a banner around it that says "God," for example. While they brainstorm, encourage pairs to think about God's commands and why they love him.

After a few minutes of brainstorming, explain that teenagers are going to follow Moses' advice by painting their symbols on each other's faces. Encourage students to think of painting the symbols on their faces as a way to show God their love for him and his commands.

Set the face paints on a table, and have partners take turns painting symbols on each other's faces. While one partner paints, the other partner should talk about how to show love for God and his commands through his or her daily life.

After kids have painted each other's faces, ask them to take turns presenting their symbols to the rest of the class and to God. Ask each person to describe how the symbol represents his or her love for God and how the symbol reminds him or her to follow God's commands.

Praise Prayers

Scripture: Psalm 19

Theme: Prayer

Experience: In this **creative movement** and **prayer of invocation,** teenagers will create motions to express a prayer to God.

Preparation: You'll need Bibles.

Worship

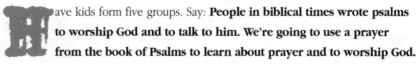

ave kids form five groups. Say: **People in biblical times wrote psalms to worship God and to talk to him. We're going to use a prayer from the book of Psalms to learn about prayer and to worship God.**

Assign the first group Psalm 19:1-4a (through the words "ends of the world"); the second group Psalm 19:4b-6 (beginning with the words "In the heavens"); the third group Psalm 19:7-8; the fourth group Psalm 19:9-11; and the fifth group Psalm 19:12-14. Have groups read their verses and discuss these questions:

- **What is the purpose of these verses?**
- **What do these verses say about God?**
- **What do these verses say about the author?**

After a few minutes of discussion, ask each group—in order from Group 1 to Group 5—to summarize the Scripture and its purpose. Then ask:

- **What does this psalm and our discussion tell you about prayer?**
- **Does Psalm 19 show us the only way to pray? Explain.**

Say: **Psalm 19 is a wonderful example of prayer, but we can talk to God in very personal ways. We're going to pray and worship God in our own way while using the words from Psalm 19.**

Many cultures use movement to express thoughts, words, and stories. Psalm 19 is a very descriptive prayer, so each group is going to create motions to represent its section of the psalm. Then we'll present our prayer to God using both the words of Psalm 19 and your motions.

Give groups at least five minutes to create motions for their sections of the psalm. Circulate as groups work to give suggestions and help as needed.

Afterward have the groups stand in order. Remind teenagers that they're presenting a prayer to God to worship him. Then have each group present its motions while reading aloud the words. Then ask:

- **What did this experience teach you about prayer?**
- **How can you incorporate some of what you learned into your own prayer life?**

Finally, have youth spend a few minutes in personal prayer to God, following the example set in Psalm 19 and incorporating what they learned about prayer.

The Path of Wisdom

Scripture: Proverbs 2

Theme: God's Wisdom

Experience: In this **creative writing experience** and **prayer of petition**, teenagers will think of situations about which they need God's wisdom, and will follow a path to seek God's wisdom.

Preparation: You'll need Bibles, markers, tape, and seven sheets of newsprint. Before this experience, write one of the following questions on each of six sheets of newsprint:

- About what situation do I need God's wisdom?
- How can I accept God's words and store up God's commands within me?
- How can I turn my ear to wisdom?
- How can I apply my heart to understanding?
- How can I call out for insight and cry aloud for understanding?
- How can I look for wisdom and search for it as hidden treasure?

    On the last sheet of newsprint write "Proverbs 2:9-22." Tape the sheets of newsprint in order on the floor around the room so teenagers can move from the first sheet to the last.

Worship

Have teenagers form pairs to read Proverbs 2:1-8. Then have pairs discuss these questions:

- **According to this Scripture, what is wisdom?**
- **What can God's wisdom do for you?**
- **What are God's promises to you when you ask him for wisdom?**
- **What's it like to search for wisdom?**

Say: **You're going to search for wisdom today by following a path. Think about following this path as if you're walking with God. At each sheet of newsprint, think about the wisdom God offers. You can follow the path with your partner, but each of you must answer the questions along the path for yourselves.** Distribute markers, and show youth the path of newsprint questions you prepared. Explain that when pairs get to the last sheet, they should wait quietly for everyone else.

Have pairs begin following the path, stopping to write answers at each sheet of newsprint. As teenagers work, circulate to offer clarification if necessary, and remind teenagers to think about God and his wisdom.

When everyone has gathered at the last sheet of newsprint, have volunteers read aloud the different answers to each question along the newsprint path. Then have students read Proverbs 2:9-22. Ask:

- **What are some of the benefits of wisdom?**
- **What did you learn about seeking God's wisdom?**
- **What different ways will you seek God's wisdom for the situation you wrote about?**

On the last sheet of newsprint, have students write prayers to God, asking for wisdom for personal situations and telling how they will seek wisdom.

Sealed Commitments

Scripture: Matthew 5:14-16

Theme: Good Deeds

Experience: In this **act of commitment**, teenagers will think about specific ways of being light to the world and will seal their commitments with wax.

Preparation: You'll need a Bible, a candle, a match, newsprint, markers, and tape.

Worship

Set a candle in the middle of the floor, and have everyone sit in a circle around it. Light the candle, then turn out the lights. Ask a volunteer to read aloud Matthew 5:14-16 by candlelight. Ask:

- **How are good deeds like light?**
- **According to this passage, what's the purpose of doing good deeds?**
- **What does it mean to you that you're to be the light of the world?**
- **How can you let your light shine?**

Have everyone spend a few moments talking to God about what it means to them that they're God's light and how they can shine God's light in the world.

After a few minutes, turn on the lights again. Set aside the candle—but don't blow it out—and set a sheet of newsprint and several markers in the middle of the circle. Say: **I'd like you to make a commitment to God about a specific way you'll shine God's light to the world. Then, just as the Bible says, others will praise God for what you do.**

In the middle of the newsprint, write, "I'll shine God's light to the world by..." Then tell youth that they can write their commitments on the newsprint.

When everyone has finished, drip a few drops of melted candle wax next to each person's written commitment. Have each person wait a few moments for the wax to cool and then press their index fingers into the wax to seal their commitments. After everyone has imprinted the wax, pray to thank God for the opportunity to be light to the world; ask God to bless the students' commitments so that people will praise God.

Tape the sheet of newsprint to a wall as a reminder to students to carry out the commitments they made to God.

Balloon Bouquets

Scripture: Romans 5:1-5

Theme: Hope

Experience: In this **sharing time** and **act of praise**, teenagers will write on balloons the reasons for their hope and will present their balloons to God.

Preparation: You'll need Bibles, balloons, markers, scissors, and ribbon.

Worship

Ask teenagers to define and describe hope. Then ask them to call out things that make them feel hopeful. Every time someone calls out a reason for hope, toss that person a balloon to blow up and tie off. Then ask:

• **How do balloons remind you of hopeful things?**

• **How is the feeling of hope similar to a balloon being blown up?**

Say: **Balloons are often used at celebrations because they're colorful and fun. They remind us of happy, fun times. The way we fill them with air is a lot like the way we feel when we're filled with the happiness hope brings.**

Have youth form pairs, and distribute Bibles. Have pairs read Romans 5:1-5, paying close attention to what the Scripture teaches about hope. Then have pairs work together to restate the Scripture in their own words. After a few minutes, ask:

- **What hope do Christians have?**
- **Why does being justified through faith bring hope?**
- **What's your response to that hope?**
- **When have you seen hope grow through suffering, perseverance, and character?**

Ask volunteers to share real-life examples of how people's hope in God has grown through suffering, perseverance, and character. For example, someone might describe how his or her father was laid off, which led him to depend on God through several months of less-than-ideal work until his character changed from pride to reliance on God. If possible, start this time of sharing with a story from your own life.

Afterward, say: **God does so many wonderful things for our hope. God helps us turn our bad times into hopeful times, and God justifies us if we have faith so we can be at peace with him and live in heaven someday. God gives us hope in wonderful ways. Let's praise God for the hope he gives us.**

Distribute markers, and give a balloon to anyone who doesn't already have one. Explain that each person should write on a balloon a note to God, praising God for something that makes him or her hopeful. Then distribute lengths of ribbon so students can tie all their balloons together.

Present the balloon bouquet of praise to God in class by having each person pray, "I praise you, God, for..." and then reading the note from his or her balloon. Also present the balloon bouquet to God during a regular worship service, if possible.

Commissioned to Love

Scripture: Romans 13:8-12

Theme: Loving Others

Experience: In this creative writing experience and commissioning, teenagers will discuss how they can better love others, and will write letters encouraging one another to share God's love with others.

Preparation: You'll need a Bible, paper, pens, envelopes, and postage stamps.

Worship

ave students silently think of people they have trouble loving, from a specific person to an entire group of people. Then have students think about why they have trouble loving those people.

Ask a volunteer to read aloud Romans 13:8-12. Ask:

• **What does it mean that loving one another is to be our only continuing debt?**

• **What's your response to Paul's words about the present time and waking from slumber?**

• **Why is it difficult to love others?**

• **How does loving others—especially those we have trouble loving—show that we love God?**

• **How might you treat differently the people you have trouble loving if you loved them as you love yourself?**

Have teenagers form pairs. Ask pairs to tell each other and God about the people they have trouble loving and why they have trouble loving those people. Encourage pairs to include God in their conversations through prayer or "This is what I'd say to God" discussions. Also encourage pairs to listen to their partners with loving hearts, without judgment or a desire to gossip.

After a few minutes of sharing, distribute envelopes, paper, pens, and postage stamps. Have each student write a letter to his or her partner. Explain that the letters should include the following:

• one or two ideas about how partners can lovingly treat the people they have trouble loving,

• a statement challenging and commissioning their partners to love others as they love themselves, and

• a prayer their partners can pray to God about the situation.

Encourage teenagers to write the letters as if writing as agents of God, commissioning their partners to do God's will. When everyone has finished writing, have students put the letters in the envelopes, stamp the envelopes, and address the envelopes to their partners. Collect the envelopes, and mail them later in the week.

The Knowledge of God

Scripture: Ephesians 1:17-21

Theme: Knowing God

Experience: In this **sharing time** and **prayer of intercession**, teenagers will create prayers for one another that ask God to help them know him better.

Preparation: You'll need Bibles, paper, pens, scissors, and yarn.

Worship

ave teenagers form trios, and distribute a length of yarn to each person. Explain that they are to somehow manipulate the pieces of yarn to represent how well they know others listed below. Ask teenagers to use their pieces of yarn to figuratively show how well they know

- the strangers they meet on the street,
- their best friends, and
- their teachers at school,
- their family members.

Finally, ask trios to discuss how well they feel like they know God.

Distribute Bibles, and have trios read Ephesians 1:17-21. Then have trios discuss these questions:

- **What does this Scripture tell you about God?**
- **What does this Scripture tell you about knowing God?**
- **What does this prayer tell you about God's desire to know you?**

Ask each person to use the yarn to show how much they feel like God loves him or her. Then ask each person to use the yarn to show how much the Scripture says God loves him or her. Have trios discuss these questions:

- **What's your response to the power and blessings God makes available to those who know him?**
- **How do you seek to know God better?**

Say: **It's easy for us to forget just how much God wants us to know him. But God's love is so vast that he not only sent Jesus to die on the cross to save us, but he also wants to draw us into an intimate friendship with him.**

Distribute paper and pens, then say: **Paul's prayer for the Ephesians was that they understand how much God wanted to bless them. Using Paul's prayer as a blueprint, I want each trio member to pray for another trio member. Your prayers should praise God for how much he wants to know that person and should encourage that person to recognize God's immense love for him or her.**

Tell students that they can use Paul's prayer verbatim or they can use the paper and pens to create their own prayers. Be sure each person prays and that each person is prayed for.

Afterward, encourage students to use their pieces of yarn to mark Ephesians 1:17-21 so they can remind themselves of God's love whenever they need to.

How to Change the World

Scripture: Colossians 3:1-14

Theme: Holy Living

Experience: In this **creative reading**, teenagers will compare newspaper stories to Scripture to determine the difference following God can make.

Preparation: You'll need Bibles and newspapers or news magazines.

Worship

Have students form three groups, and give each group several newspapers or news magazines. Say: **These publications help us keep tabs on what's going on in the world. When we read, we find out that our world is neck-deep in lots of problems. It is certainly not where God would want it to be.**

Distribute Bibles. Say: **We can easily find out what God has in mind for the way we should live our lives. Let's see what God has to say about how he'd like people in the world to be living.**

Assign the first group Colossians 3:1-4; the second group Colossians 3:5-11; and the third group Colossians 3:12-14. Explain that each group will prepare a creative reading presentation to compare what's happening in our world to what God would like to be happening in our world. For example, a group might read several headlines from a newspaper, each followed by a section of the group's Scripture that supports or condemns what the headline reports. Tell students that they'll be presenting their creative readings to God.

Give groups about ten minutes to work. Circulate as groups work to offer help as needed. When groups are ready, have them stand in order from Group 1 to Group 3. Then have groups present their creative readings to God.

Applaud the presentations, then have groups discuss these questions:

• **Which is better: our world as it is or our world as it could be if people followed God's Word? Explain.**

• **What would the world be like if people obeyed God?**

• **How can you make a difference by obeying God?**

Close by praying that the students make a difference in the world by subscribing not to the newspapers' worldview, but to God's Word.

Believing Over Time

Scripture: 1 Peter 1:3-9
Theme: Faith
Experience: In this **declaration of faith**, teenagers will create a group
time line that reflects their experiences with faith.
Preparation: You'll need Bibles, tape, newsprint, and markers.

Worship

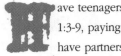ave teenagers form pairs, and distribute Bibles. Ask pairs to read 1 Peter
1:3-9, paying close attention to what the Scripture says about faith. Then
have partners discuss these questions:

• **What does this Scripture say about faith?**
• **Why are we to have faith?**
• **How would you define faith?**
• **What are the benefits of having faith?**

As pairs are discussing the questions, tape a long sheet of newsprint horizontally
to a wall. At one end, write the words "You were born." Then draw a long horizontal
line to the other end. At that end, write "Today." Place markers beneath the newsprint.

Say: **This Scripture says a lot about faith—that it shields us with God's
power, that it's strengthened when we suffer, that it will bring us glory and
salvation someday. Today we're going to declare our faith to others and to
God by creating a group time line about our experiences with faith.**

Have pairs discuss any personal experiences they've had with faith. The
Scripture can direct students to what faith is and the circumstances under which
they may have experienced it. For example, students might remember really feeling God's presence at a concert, think about when they first believed in God, or
realize that their faith grew during a difficult time. Each time someone thinks of an
experience with faith, have him or her write it on the time line.

After everyone has finished, ask a few volunteers to further declare their faith
by describing their experiences to the group and to God. Encourage students to
read other people's entries on the time line. Then close by thanking God for sharing himself with the students.

The Song of Growth in Christ

Scripture: 2 Peter 1:3-8

Theme: Spiritual Growth

Experience: In this **creative writing experience** and **music experience,** teenagers will create a song to reflect the steps of spiritual growth.

Preparation: You'll need a Bible, paper, and pencils.

Worship

sk volunteers to describe what they think spiritual growth is and how to grow spiritually. Then say: **Spiritual growth is a process that Peter described in the Bible. As I read, think about the beginning of spiritual growth and the process.**

Read aloud 2 Peter 1:3-8. Then ask:

- **How do God's gifts and promises affect our faith?**
- **How do we build on faith to grow spiritually?**
- **What are some benefits of growing spiritually?**

Say: **Spiritual growth is kind of like a song. We start with one verse, then add another and another. You're going to write a song for God that reflects the different stages of spiritual growth Peter wrote about. Each verse will build on the previous one to show how people grow spiritually.**

Have students form eight groups: faith, faith to goodness, goodness to knowledge, knowledge to self-control, self-control to perseverance, perseverance to godliness, godliness to kindness, and kindness to love. (If you have fewer than sixteen people, it's OK to have some groups write more than one verse.) Explain that each group will write a verse to describe not only how a person might grow from one stage to the next, but also why that attribute is spiritually important.

Before groups begin, have teenagers choose a familiar tune to set their verses to. Then provide paper and pencils, and have groups write their verses.

When groups have finished, tell students they're going to sing their song to God. Have groups stand in order and share their verses. Applaud their work, then ask:

- **What stage of the growth process do you think you're in?**
- **How might you work on growing spiritually?**

Encourage students to remember the song as they pursue spiritual growth.

The Great Commissioning

Scripture: Matthew 28:18-20

Theme: Sharing Faith

Experience: In this **commissioning** and **music experience**, teenagers will be commissioned to be the light of the world.

Preparation: You'll need one candle for each participant, a dramatic slide show (or video or collection of pictures) of a mix of people from around the world, and a worship band.

Worship

Begin the worship session by leading kids in singing songs of worship to God. Afterward, show a slide show (or video, or a collection of pictures) to the group with soft music playing in the background. The pictures can be focused on a certain part of the world (perhaps a place that someone in your church will be going to on a missions trip), all over the world (perhaps from Life magazine), or even snapshots of people in your town.

After viewing the pictures, say: **People all over desperately need to hear of the peace and love of Christ. It is our job to tell them.**

Read Matthew 28:18-20. Ask:

- **Why would people be better off after hearing about Christ?**
- **What do we have that others don't?**
- **What would hold me back from sharing with others about Christ?**
- **In what ways can you share the love of God with others?**

Give a candle to each student and dim the lights. Light your candle and say: **Christ was the light of the world. His disciples spread his message to those around them, and those around them shared with others. It became a chain reaction. You became part of that chain reaction and are entrusted with his Word. Go and be a light to the world. Don't let his Word stop with you.**

Light the candle of the person next to you. Have that person light somebody else's candle and watch as everybody's candle eventually becomes lit.

Close by praying that we can be lights in the world. Allow kids to take their candles home as reminders to fulfill God's commission to be a light to the world.

Proclamations of Praise

Scripture: Psalm 136

Theme: Praising God

Experience: In this **drama presentation**, teenagers will write and perform a Readers Theater on their perception of God.

Preparation: You'll need pens, and a copy of the "My God" script (pp. 56-57) for each student.

Worship

To begin, have the whole group join in a simple Readers Theater based on Psalm 136. Have kids stand. You read the first part of each verse, and have kids respond by saying, "His love endures forever." Encourage kids to focus on worshipping God as they listen and respond.

Afterward, have the students get into groups of three.

Say: **Proclaiming our worship to God is important. Today we are all going to proclaim worship to God by using our skills as writers and actors. Don't worry, it doesn't require any major talent. The script I'll provide has blanks, and you just have to fill them in and then read it to the group.**

Distribute the "My God" scripts (pp. 56-57) to the students, along with pens.

Say: **You can choose among your group who wants to be Green, Blue, or Yellow. Then fill in the appropriate blanks and practice reading it before you read before the group. It's not an "acting out" drama, but a Readers Theater.**

Oversee and help as they write and practice. If two people in one group want to put the same word in their blanks, that's OK. Repetition can add to the drama.

When groups are ready, have them take turns presenting their Readers Theater to the group. After each presentation, have the rest of the group applaud by saying in unison: "His love endures forever!"

The Evidence of Creation

Scripture: Psalm 65

Theme: Creation

Experience: In this **artistic experience** and **prayer of thanksgiving,** students will cut out pictures of creation that best reveal God's

My God

Green: My God

Blue: A creative work by

Green: _____ (your name)

Blue: _____ (your name)

Yellow: _____ (your name).

Blue: _____ (your favorite worship song title)

Yellow: _____ (your favorite worship song title)

Green: _____ (your favorite worship song title)

Blue: I call him _____ (name of God)

Green: _____ (name of God)

Yellow: _____ (name of God)

All: _____ (name of God).

Yellow: He is _____ (adjective of God), _____ (adjective of God),

Blue: and _____ (adjective of God).

Green: He is my _____ (role of God) when I _____ (activity that you do).

Yellow: He is my _____ (role of God) when I _____ (activity that you do).

All: He is _____ (role of God).

Yellow: I met him when I was _____ (age you became a Christian)

Blue: _____ (age you became a Christian)

Green: _____ (age you became a Christian).

Yellow: To know God more, I _____ (activity you do to know God better)

Blue: _____ (activity you do to know God better)

Green: _____ (activity you do to know God better).

Blue: We come before him

All: _____ (how you approach God).

Yellow: If I could ask him one question, I would ask:

Green: _____ (question for God)

Blue: _____ (question for God)

Yellow: _____ (question for God).

Green: But even if I don't know the answer now,

All: That's OK.

Green: His _____ (attribute of God) surrounds me.

Blue: His _____ (attribute of God) overwhelms me.

Yellow: His _____ (attribute of God) envelops me.

Blue: He is God.

Green: He is God.

Yellow: He is God.

All: He is God.

existence to them.

Preparation: You'll need one piece of poster board for each group of four or five, glue, and magazines (National Geographic, Life, or other magazines that deal with travel, astronomy, or nature).

Worship

ay: **God reveals himself in many ways. Some people look to Scripture, some to science and philosophy, and some just look at the lives of their friends who claim to be changed by God. In all those ways, people can realize that God exists. Another common path is creation. Sometimes, just looking at God's amazing creation, we must say, "There is a God."**

Ask volunteers to take turns reading successive verses of Psalm 65. Then say: **God says creation worships him** (verse 13). **In this activity, we're going to cut out pictures of parts of creation that reveal God's existence, and use them to make a worship collage.**

Form groups of four or five, and set out the supplies you gathered earlier. Give groups several minutes to cut and paste pictures that reveal God in some way. Afterward, have each group stand and share with the whole group what they put on their collage and how that reveals God's existence to them. Once all the groups have shared, pray together giving God thanks for his beautiful creation.

Close by having kids pray together, thanking God for specific aspects of nature that help them recognize his presence in their lives.

Personalized Praise

Scripture: Psalm 71:14-16

Theme: Praising God

Experience: In this **complete service**, teenagers will have the opportunity to create unique, personalized praises for God, and participate in a time of praise and worship.

Preparation: You'll need Bibles, paper, and pens or pencils. Use the alphabetical list of praise words to help students if they get stuck.

Worship

Read Psalm 71:14-16.

Ask:

• **What's the difference between praising God and thanking him?** After giving students a chance to answer, say: **When I thank God, I thank him for what he does. When I praise God, I tell him what I appreciate about who he is.**

Give an example using someone in your group—thanking him or her for something he or she has done for you, and then praising him or her for an attribute, such as compassion, loyalty, or wisdom. Then tell kids that in today's experience, they'll focus on worshipping God for who he is.

Say: **The Psalms are songs that were used in worship. A great number of them were praise songs. We can find praises to God throughout the Bible, but the Psalms are a good place to start looking for praises.**

Tell students to turn in their Bibles to the book of Psalms, and begin identifying attributes of God. For example, Psalm 28 lists these attributes for God: rock (verse 1); merciful (verse 2); just (verse 4); strength, shield, and helper (verse 7); fortress of salvation (verse 8); and savior (verse 9).

Say: **Now I'd like each person to design a personal praise for God—using praises that begin with the letters of your own name. Let's just do first names.**

Give each student time to search out praises for God that begin with the letters in their names. If they have trouble, you can use the list below. When they're done, lead kids in a time of praising God.

Start by asking everyone to kneel, and then pray: **Oh God, you are...** or **Lord, I praise you because you...**Then ask students to take turns, each praising God for attributes that begin with the letters of their first names.

After the praise service, suggest that kids take their lists home and keep them to use as a personalized praise to God.

Use this list of attributes (taken from Psalms) to help kids if they get stuck:

A. awesome (89:7; 47:2); almighty (84:1); avenger (94:1)

B. blessed (72:17); beautiful (27:4); bountiful (23:1)

C. caring (8:4); Creator (95:5); constant (26:3); compassionate (111:4); comforter (71:21)

D. delightful (37:4); deliverer (56:13); defender (28:1); dedicated (55:17)

E. everlasting (90:2); enduring (135:13); eternal (111:10)

F. forgiving (25:7); faithful (25:10); fortress (91:2); friend (25:14)

G. good (30:5); gracious (116:5); great (8:1); guide (23:3)

H. holy (99:5); healer (30:2); hope (25:21)

I. immortal (44:8); invisible (1 Timothy 1:17); invincible (44:7); indispensable (39:7); infallible (19:7-12)

J. just (111:7); joyful (92:4); judge (96:13)

K. kind (106:7); king (95:3); knowing (92:5)

L. loving (62:12); leader (107:7); light (27:1); liberator (31:8)

M. merciful (31:9); mighty (89:8); marvelous (98:1); maker (95:6); majestic (110:3)

N. near (119:151); never-ending (48:14)

O. omnipresent (139:7-8)

P. perfect (19:7); protector (25:20); perceptive (139:2); provider (111:5); powerful (106:8)

Q. quick (71:12); qualified (24:1)

R. rescuer (31:2); refuge (31:4); righteous (31:1); redeemer (111:9); ruler (99:1); rock (62:2, 7)

S. strong (62:11); shepherd (23:1); salvation (27:1)

T. teacher (25:4); tenderhearted (25:7); truthful (25:5)

U. understanding (147:5); unfailing (107:31)

V. victorious (24:8); vindicator (17:2)

W. wise (19:7); wonderful (9:1); worthy (18:3); with us (46:11); watchful (141:3)

X. eXcellent (76:4); eXalted (113:4)

Y. yielding (107:37); yours (76:11)

Z. zealous (Numbers 25:11)

Getting Real With Jesus

Scripture: John 4:5-42

Theme: Knowing Jesus

Experience: In this **drama presentation** and **meditation**, teenagers will explore a Bible story to see how a real Jesus treated real people, then spend time in silence, worshipping God in spirit and truth.

Preparation: You'll need Bibles, and one copy of the "Silent Questions" handout (p. 63) for each student.

Worship

This worship experience will help kids get in touch with how the people felt actually being with Jesus, and what it means to worship God in spirit and truth.

First, guide kids to read the story found in John 4:5-42. Since it's fairly long, it will help if you involve students in the reading. Here's how:

You can be the narrator. You'll need volunteers from the group to act as disciples, Jesus, the woman, and the townspeople. Involve all of the group members if you can. Select a place in your room to be the "well" and another place to be the "town." Ask actors to enter and exit as their characters are mentioned, and to read the direct quotes from the Bible as you come to them.

To help make the story real for kids, stop and read the following descriptive background comments as you "act" through the passage together.

After verse 7, say: **Jacob's well was a historic site even then.**

After verse 9, say: **Jews hated Samaritans mostly because the Samaritans practiced a mongrel type religion mixing pure worship of God with worship of the false god, Baal. In the time of Nehemiah, the Samaritans opposed the Jews in the rebuilding of the walls of Jerusalem. By the time of Jesus, quite a strong rivalry and hatred existed between the Jews and Samaritans. The woman represents this hated race—and she was immoral on top of that.**

After verse 18, say: **Jesus says an odd thing about "living water" and in the next verse, the woman immediately seizes on it, seemingly without question. Then she and Jesus have this strange conversation about her marital and sexual background. This is not the kind of conversation we consider "normal."**

After verse 20, say: **The debate over where people should worship God was a really sore point between the Jews and Samaritans. The Samaritans based their belief on the historical fact that when Moses led the Jews into the Promised Land, he had tribes divided, half on Mount Ebal and half on Mount Gerizim. On Mount Gerizim the blessings of God were pronounced so that should be the center of worship. The Jews believed Jerusalem should be the center of worship because Solomon had been commissioned by God to build the temple there. The controversy was endless. Jesus didn't get into it with her.**

Following the dramatic reading, help kids fully understand the story by discussing these questions:

• **What was Jesus trying to tell us about himself by talking to this "second-class," immoral woman?**

• **What did Jesus mean when he said we should worship "in spirit and truth"?**

• **What do you think happened with the woman and the man she was living with following her encounter with Jesus?**

• **What was it about Jesus that impressed the townspeople so much?**

• **How would you have felt if, instead of the woman, Jesus had met you at the well?**

Say: **We're going to spend some time meeting with Jesus "in spirit and truth"—and in absolute silence. I'd like to ask you to spend ten minutes completely alone with Jesus. Seek to get in touch with his Spirit. Think about this Scripture, and what it might have felt like to spend time with Jesus at the well—all by yourself. Be completely open and vulnerable before him. Allow yourself to be completely truthful. Don't hold back anything from him.**

Have kids find a private place on the floor as far away from others as possible. Give each person a copy of the "Silent Questions" handout (p. 63). Tell kids to use the questions on the handout to help them focus their time on meeting with Jesus.

Afterward, ask kids to share their experiences during this time of silent worship.

Ambassadors for Christ

Scripture: 2 Corinthians 5:17-20

Theme: Sharing Faith

Experience: In this creative writing experience and declaration of faith, teenagers will write speeches as ambassadors for Christ to present as testimony to who he is.

Preparation: You'll need Bibles, pens or pencils, and paper.

Worship

sk volunteers to read aloud 2 Corinthians 5:17-20. Then ask the group these questions:

• **What's an ambassador?**

Silent Questions

As you pray silently, tell Jesus how you would respond to each of the questions below:

1. How would you feel if Jesus had met you at the well and asked you for a drink?

2. Do you believe Jesus is present with you right now? Why or why not?

3. What are three questions about your life that you would like Jesus to answer for you?

4. What questions do you think Jesus would want to ask you?

5. More than anything, what do you want Jesus to do for you?

6. What do you think Jesus wants you to do for him?

• **What does it mean to be an ambassador for God?**

Have kids form trios. Then say: **Congratulations! You've just been assigned a position in the Office of Foreign Affairs in the Kingdom of God. You're going to be an ambassador to a non-Christian land. To prepare for your new job, you have to write your inaugural speech for the people of this foreign land. In your trios, decide who will play the role of ambassador. The rest of you are speech writers. In your trios, write a speech as if you're an ambassador for Christ and are assigned to show how great he is and why people everywhere should believe in him.**

Give trios time to create their speeches. When they're ready, lead kids in a time of worship, using the speeches to glorify God for who he is. Have each ambassador share a speech with the whole group.

After the worship time, ask:

• **What does it mean to be an ambassador for Christ in your daily life?**

• **How can you use what you wrote in these speeches to inspire you to share Christ with your friends and family members?**

Close with prayer, asking God to show each one how Jesus would have them be ambassadors for him in their daily lives.

Ask, Seek, Knock

Scripture: Psalm 18; Matthew 7:7-12

Theme: God's Goodness

Experience: In this **drama presentation** and **prayer of petition**, kids will perform a Readers Theater based on Matthew 7:7-12, then use Psalm 18 as a guide in prayer.

Preparation: You'll need Bibles, and a copy of the "Ask, Seek, Knock" script (pp. 66-67) for each person.

Worship

As kids enter, give each person a copy of the "Ask, Seek, Knock" script (pp. 66-67). When everyone has arrived, form six groups, and assign each group one of the "student" roles. Tell kids they're going to perform the skit as a Readers Theater. They'll read their parts in unison, using their voices alone to create the drama.

After the drama, read aloud Matthew 7:7-12. Then ask:

- **What do you think God means when he says he'll give us what we ask for?**
- **What kind of good gifts does God want us to have?**
- **What kind of things do we ask God for?**
- **What kind of things should we ask for?**

Close by asking kids to pray part of Psalm 18—about God's desire to answer our prayers and heal our lives. Do this by asking kids to open their Bibles to Psalm 18. Assign the following verses: 2, 3, 16, 17, 18, 19, 25, 26, 27, 28, 29, 30, 31, 32, 43, 46, 47, 48, 49. It's OK if some kids are assigned more than one verse.

Tell kids that praying a psalm means that we are directing the psalm to God, rather than just reading it. Say: **This psalm expresses love toward God, praise, thanksgiving for safety and healing, reliance on God, and humility toward God. As you pray through the verses I've assigned, think of specific things in your lives that relate to what you're reading.**

You start by reading verse 1. Then ask kids to "pray" their assigned verse(s) in turn until you have completed the psalm.

The Coming of Christ

Scripture: Isaiah 40:3-5

Theme: Advent

Experience: In this **artistic experience** and **prayer of confession**, teenagers will prepare their hearts and lives for the coming of Christ.

Preparation: You'll need Bibles, poster board, markers or poster paints in a variety of colors, masking tape, one copy of the "Preparing My Heart" handout (p. 69) for each student, pens or pencils, and a CD player with a CD of soft, reflective music (optional).

Worship

ay: **This is the season of Advent; the season of preparing our hearts and lives for Christ's birth.** Read Isaiah 40:3-5 aloud, and say: **This Scripture was written many years before Christ's birth, and it prophesied preparations which God's people would make. We can also use it to help us prepare.**

Have teenagers form three groups, and make sure each group has a Bible, a piece of poster board, and markers or poster paints. Assign each group one of the

Ask, Seek, Knock

Student 1: "Ask and it will be given to you;"

Student 2: Could I please have one?

Student 1: "...seek and you will find;"

Student 3: I can't find it anywhere. I know it was here somewhere. Oh, I hate to lose things. Nope, it's not here. Nope, not there. Oh, please, does anyone know where it is?

Student 1: Try looking over there.

Student 3: Hey, thanks!

Student 1: "...knock and the door will be opened to you."

Student 4: Anyone home?

Student 1: Will someone please get the door?

Student 4: I'm just waiting around here.

Student 1: "For everyone who asks receives;"

Student 2: Look! I got it. Isn't it great?

Student 1: "...he who seeks finds;"

Student 3: I found it! Look!

Student 1: "...and to him who knocks, the door will be opened."

Student 4: Hey—hello. How are you doing?

Student 1: "Which of you, if his son asks for bread, will give him a stone?"

Student 5: Daddy, can I have some bread? Please, please, please? I'm so HUNGRY. Need bread. Please?

Student 1: Here, take this rock.

Student 5: What am I supposed to do with a rock? I'm hungry.

Student 1: "Or if he asks for a fish, will give him a snake?"

Student 5: OK. How about a fish? If you don't have any bread, can I have a fish?

Student 1: No. But here's a nice snake.

Student 5: Ahh! Snake! Snake! Look out everybody. It's a snake!

Student 1: "If you, then, though you are evil, know how to give good gifts to your children,"...I was just kidding. Here's a tuna fish sandwich.

Student 5: Thanks, Dad.

Student 1: "...how much more will your Father in heaven give good gifts to those who ask him!"

Student 6: Wow! Gifts for me?

Student 4: Your Father in heaven wants you to have good gifts.

Student 6: Awesome!

Student 1: "So in everything, do to others what you would have them do to you,"

Student 6: So, I guess I need to give this to someone who needs it more than me, huh?

Student 1: "...for this sums up the Law and the Prophets."

Student 3: That's all, folks.

Student 5: What are we going to do with this rock and this snake?

verses in the passage. Have each group create an illustration of its assigned verse on the poster board, including the text and verse reference.

When groups are finished illustrating their verses, have them create three different "prayer stations" by taping their illustrations on three different walls in the room.

Give each student a "Preparing My Heart" handout (p. 69) and a pen or pencil. Say: **Now I'd like you to ask God for his help to prepare your life for Christ's coming. Travel to one prayer station at a time; it doesn't matter where you start. When you're at a station, sit by yourself and look at the illustration. Then, in an attitude of prayer, write your answer to the question on your handout for that station. Take your time and don't talk to anyone else; this is a time for you to spend with God.**

Play soft, reflective music while students move from station to station.

The One and Only God

Scripture: Joshua 24:19-27

Theme: Following God

Experience: In this **act of commitment**, teenagers will commit to following only God.

Preparation: You'll need a Bible, slips of paper, pens or pencils, an ink pad, paper towels, and a large rock.

Worship

ave teenagers sit in a circle and place the large rock in the center of the circle. Give each teenager a slip of paper and a pen or pencil.

Read Joshua 24:19-27 aloud. Say: **In this passage, Joshua challenged the Israelites to stop following other gods and to love and serve only the one true God. I'm challenging you today to do the same thing. When I'm finished giving the instructions, I'd like you to think for a moment about what god you sometimes serve instead of the one true God. This may be the god of money or the god of friends' opinions. Write your false god on your slip of paper. Then bring your slip of paper to the middle of the circle and leave it under the rock.**

When students have finished, say: **We've placed all of our slips of paper under the rock. In the same way, all of our false gods are under the one true God. His power is greater than the power of any of our false gods. To**

Preparing My Heart

Station 1

- What highway in your life needs to be made straight for God to travel on? Write a brief prayer here.

Station 2

- What rugged and rough places in your heart do you need God's help to smooth out? Write a brief prayer here.

Station 3

- How might the glory of the Lord be revealed to you personally? Write a brief prayer here.

help us commit to following only the one true God and not our false gods, I'm going to pass the rock around, along with an ink pad. When it comes to you, I'd like you to leave your fingerprint on it and say a brief prayer, asking God to use his power to help you reject false gods.

When the rock has been passed all the way around the circle, distribute paper towels so kids can clean the ink off their fingers. Then hold up the rock and say: **In the same way that Joshua's rock served as a witness to the Israelites' commitment to God, so will this rock serve as a witness to our commitment. I'll leave this rock in our room, and every time you see it, it will remind you of your commitment to love and serve only God.**

Stars for God

Scripture: Philippians 2:14-16
Theme: Sharing Faith
Experience: In this **act of commitment**, teenagers will discover ways they can share Christ with others through the way they live their lives.
Preparation: You'll need a Bible, newsprint, markers, masking tape, and several star stickers for each person.

Worship

Have students form trios. Give each trio six to nine star stickers, newsprint, and markers. Read Philippians 2:14-16 aloud and ask:
• **What does it mean to "shine like stars in the universe"?**
• **What are some ways we can shine our light for others?**
• **How can the way we choose to live our lives help others find Christ?**
• **Why should we share Christ's light with other people?**

Have each trio brainstorm ways they can show others the way to Christ using light and write them down on their newsprint. For example, they may think of changing light bulbs for a senior citizen who has a hard time reaching them, or showing the "light" of a great big smile to someone who's grouchy or sad. When each trio has come up with several things, have trios tape their newsprint to the wall and share their ideas with the whole group. Ask each person to choose one service idea and carry it out during the next week. Give two or three star stickers to each group member. Challenge them to give a star sticker to the person or people they are serving and tell them about the true light of their lives—Jesus Christ.

Have trios close together with a STAR prayer. First, each trio member shares with God (either aloud or silently) the way he or she chose to **S**erve God during the coming week. Next, each person shares a reason he or she is **T**hankful for God's presence in the universe. Then each person shares a reason he or she **A**dores and worships God. Finally, each person can close with an expression of **R**ejoicing in God's presence.

The Beautiful Attitudes

Scripture: Matthew 5:1-12
Theme: Developing Character
Experience: In this **drama presentation** and **prayer of thanksgiving,** teenagers will demonstrate the Beatitudes.
Preparation: You'll need Bibles, pens or pencils, paper, and index cards.

Worship

Begin by reading aloud Matthew 5:1-12 to the students. Say: **This passage tells us how a Christian looks and acts. Now let's learn about this passage in a little more depth.**

Have teenagers form improv teams of three or four. Assign each team one or two verses from the passage, depending on class size. Make sure each team has a Bible. Say: **You'll need to read through your assigned verses very carefully. Then discuss in your group what you think they mean. You'll need to be prepared to explain them to the rest of the group. You'll be doing your explanations improv style, so you may want to write out your explanations ahead of time so they're very clear in your minds.** Provide pencils and paper for teams to write their explanations.

Give groups a few minutes to do this. You may want to circulate among the groups to give them ideas. Then say: **Now it's time for your presentations. I'll call you up in order of your verses. You'll need to stand shoulder-to-shoulder with your teammates. Someone in the audience will call out a number between one and ten. That number will represent the number of words each person can say at a time in sharing the message of your group's verses. For example, if someone calls out "three," each person can say just three words**

at a time. You will speak in order from right to left in your group.

After each group shares its verse or verses, lead the "audience" in applause. Then discuss briefly with the whole group what they think the verses mean to their lives.

Ask each person to choose the Beatitude that they most relate to. Give each person an index card and a pen or pencil. Have kids write a short prayer to God in which they tell him how they live out this Beatitude in their daily life and thank God for the gift that goes along with that Beatitude.

God Knows You

Scripture: Psalm 139:1-4
Theme: God's Understanding
Experience: In this **creative movement**, teenagers will create "statues" to show how God knows them.
Preparation: You'll need Bibles.

Worship

ive each person a Bible, and read Psalm 139:1-4 aloud. Say: **God knows us even better than we know ourselves. He knows everything we think and feel—we can't hide anything from him.**

Have each student choose his or her favorite verse from the passage and then have students form drama troupes, made up of students who chose the same verse.

Say: **Now, in your group, I'd like you to create a freeze-frame statue to express the overall message of your verse as an act of worship to God. Make sure everyone in your group is included in your statue.**

Give students a few minutes to create their statues and then have them share their creations in order as an act of worship.

Giving Your Burdens to Jesus

Scripture: Philippians 4:6-8
Theme: Trusting God
Experience: In this **artistic experience** and **prayer of petition**, kids will use their artistic talents to pray for situations that are causing anxieties in their lives.

Preparation: You'll need Bibles, sheets of sandpaper, rolls of masking tape, and varying lengths of colored yarn.

Worship

Have kids form trios, and give each trio a Bible. Have a volunteer in each trio read aloud Philippians 4:6. Ask:

- **How do you usually handle anxiety?**
- **How could prayer help you handle your anxieties?**
- **Why do you think God answers our prayers?**

Give each trio three sheets of sandpaper and a handful of varying lengths of yarn. Show kids how the yarn sticks to the sandpaper. Say: **Think of a situation that's causing you anxiety right now. Maybe you're having trouble at school, or maybe a friend or family member is sick or needs your prayers right now. Use the yarn I've given you to "draw" a picture on the sandpaper that represents the situation that's causing you anxiety. You'll have about three minutes.**

After three minutes, have kids each explain their pictures to their trio members. Then read Philippians 4:6 aloud again. Say: **The Bible says we should give all of our anxieties to God in prayer. In your groups, take turns praying for each other's situations. If you feel comfortable, pray out loud. If you'd rather, pray silently.**

When you see that kids have finished praying, say: **The Bible tells us what happens when we turn our anxieties over to God. Have a volunteer in each group read aloud Philippians 4:7-8.**

When groups are finished reading, say: **God loves us so much that he gives us his peace. Everything good comes from God, and that's what we should focus on. Even in bad situations, God is with us, comforting and protecting us. Let's praise God for his loving care.**

Have students remove the yarn from the sandpaper. Then give each trio a roll of masking tape, and have kids tape their sheets of sandpaper together end-to-end. Then have trios tape their sandpaper together to form one large sandpaper "canvas." Tape the large sandpaper canvas to the wall, and gather teenagers in front of it.

Say: **Think of how God wants to help us with our anxieties, and how he gives us his peace during tough times. Then, each of you should create a symbol with your yarn to represent your response to God for the help he gives us in difficult times.**

After a few moments, let each person add his or her yarn to the sandpaper, forming a class response of praise to God. After everyone has added to the canvas, close the worship experience with a prayer similar to this: **Dear God, thank you for letting us come to you in prayer. Thank you for caring about how we feel. Please take care of each situation we named here today. Thank you for your peace and goodness. In Jesus' name, amen.**

Our Father's Eyes

Scripture: 1 Samuel 16:1-13
Theme: God's Acceptance
Experience: In this **drama presentation** and **prayer of thanksgiving,** students will appreciate the difference between how God looks at us and how we look at each other.
Preparation: You'll need Bibles.

Worship

Once everyone has arrived, ask for volunteers to share what they know from the Old Testament about how David became king over Israel.

After students have shared, fill in any gaps by saying: **God called David to be king over Israel while he was still a teenager whose only experience in leadership was taking care of his father's sheep. Let's take a look at how God called David to leave the sheep and rule a nation.**

Have students open their Bibles to 1 Samuel 16:1-13. Ask for volunteers to play the following parts: God, Samuel, the elders, Jesse, Eliab, Abinadab, Shammah, David, and Jesse's other sons. If you have fewer than nine students, have one person play the part of all of Jesse's sons (except David).

Say: **As I read this Bible passage, I want each person to silently act out the character the Bible describes. Ready?**

Read aloud 1 Samuel 16:1-13 very slowly to allow students time to act out the parts. Then have students sit in a circle to discuss the following questions:

• **Do people you know judge others based on outward appearances? Explain.**

• **Has anyone ever judged you based on what you looked like? How did that make you feel?**

• **Does the way people look ever affect how you treat them? Why or why not?**

Say: **Listen again to one of the verses in the Bible passage I read earlier.** Read aloud 1 Samuel 16:7b. Ask:

• **What does it mean that God looks at our hearts?**

• **How can knowing that God cares about you personally and your "heart" help you feel better about yourself? How can it help you view others?**

Say: **Take a few moments right now to silently thank God for judging you based on what's inside, rather than what's outside.** Give students a few moments to silently pray, then close by thanking God for each person in your group and thanking him for the desire he can put in each of our hearts to learn about and follow him.

Creative Genius

Scripture: Genesis 1:1-31; 2:7, 22

Theme: Creation

Experience: In this **act of praise** and **artistic experience**, students will praise God for his amazing creation of the world.

Preparation: You'll need Bibles, a plain bedsheet (or shower curtain), packing tape, washable paint, paintbrushes, sponges, colorful markers, staplers, colored tissue paper, scissors, and construction paper.

Worship

Before class, hang a bedsheet or shower curtain on your classroom wall. Set out the art supplies you've collected. Gather students in a group in front of the sheet.

Say: **When an artist begins a new painting, he or she faces a blank canvas like this blank sheet. God, the master artist, faced the same thing before he created our world. Listen.** Read aloud Genesis 1:1. Ask:

• **What do you think it was like for God, the master artist, just before he began creating our world? What do you think he was thinking?**

• **How do you think God came up with all of the intricate parts of our universe?**

• **Do you think God had fun creating our world? Explain.**

Have students gather in groups of three or four, and give each group a Bible.

s in each group to take turns reading Genesis 1:2-31; 2:7, 22. When groups

ied reading, say: **Take a moment to think of one part of creation that you're ι eally thankful for. Then we're going to praise God by using the creativity he's given us to make a creation mural to celebrate God's gift to us.**

Give students a moment to each think of one part of creation to add to the mural. Then let students create! Encourage students to draw or paint their favorite parts of creation on the sheet. For extra fun, show them how to cut paper shapes (such as leaves, bushes, and birds) and staple them to the mural to add three-dimensional depth.

After about ten or fifteen minutes, tell students it's time to finish. Then let students describe what they added to the mural, and why that's their favorite part of creation. Then hold hands in front of the mural, and say a prayer to thank God for his incredible creativity.

Consider keeping the mural hanging in your room as a visual reminder of God's greatness, or display the mural somewhere in the church for all to enjoy.

Secret Service

Scripture: Matthew 6:1-4

Theme: Serving Others

Experience: In this **service opportunity**, students will experience doing good deeds in secret, without recognition.

Preparation: You'll need a Bible, paper, pens, envelopes, and a basket.

Worship

ather students in a circle. Read aloud Matthew 6:1-4. Then ask:

• **What is this passage talking about?**

• **Why do you think Jesus says to keep your good deeds secret?**

• **What do you think Jesus means when he says that those who boast about their good deeds have received their full reward?**

Say: **In a moment, we're going to have a time of silent prayer. As you pray, ask God to help you think of one good deed you can secretly do in the next week or two. This good deed will be strictly between you and God—you won't be telling anyone about it. And your good deed doesn't have to cost money—it can be an act of kindness or friendship. Maybe you'll tell someone about Jesus, write an encouraging note to a friend who's been** down, or help an elderly neighbor with shopping. Ready? Let's pray.

Give students a minute or two to pray. Then give each person a sheet of paper, a pen, and an envelope. Have students scatter around the room so they're sitting by themselves. Then tell students to each write a note to God, asking for his help in carrying out the good deed. Have students put their notes in their envelopes, seal the envelopes, and write their names on the outside.

Say: **I'm going to collect your sealed envelopes, and keep them here in this basket. When you've completed your good deed in the next week or two, remove your envelope from the basket and take it home as a reminder of how we can please God by doing good deeds quietly.**

God With Us

Scripture: Psalm 84

Theme: God's Presence

Experience: In this **artistic experience** and **prayer of thanksgiving,** students will discover what it means to dwell in the presence of God.

Preparation: You'll need Bibles, newsprint, and colorful markers.

Worship

ather everyone in a circle.

Ask:

• **How did you feel about coming to church today?**

• **Why is church important to you?**

Say: **Church is the place where Christians come to experience God's presence together. One writer in the Bible explained how he felt about coming into God's presence. Let's see what he said.**

Have students form groups of four, and give each group a Bible. Tell students in each group to take turns reading aloud the verses in Psalm 84. Ask:

• **Why do you think the writer of this psalm yearned to be in God's house?**

• **Read verses 1 and 2 again. What do you think these verses mean?**

• **Where does God dwell today?**

Give each group colorful markers and a sheet of newsprint. Explain that each group should first draw an outline of a church building on the newsprint. When groups have finished drawing the church building, tell students to write attributes of God that they learned about while at church. For example, they might write "loving," "forgiving," and "all-knowing."

Then have group members each draw a scene on the newsprint that depicts a time they've experienced God's presence outside of church. For example, they might draw about a time they've been afraid and God has comforted them, or a time they've felt alone and God made his presence known.

Give groups about ten minutes to draw, then have each group hang its picture on the wall. Let each group member explain what he or she has drawn. Then have each group read aloud, in unison, Psalm 84:11-12. Close with a large-group prayer, thanking God and praising him for his presence at all times and in all situations.

Abide in the Vine

Scripture: John 15:1-12

Theme: Knowing Jesus

Experience: In this **artistic experience**, teenagers will create and present skits, cheers, poems, or songs that illustrate John 15:1-12.

Preparation: You'll need Bibles. If possible, locate a living vine with branches to use in the illustration.

Worship

sk volunteers to read aloud John 15:1-12. Then say: **As I read the stories Jesus told, I can imagine him walking around the countryside with his disciples and teaching them by using examples that he saw around him.**

When Jesus told the story we just read, he and his disciples were in the upper room of a place where they often spent time together. I can imagine them reclining around the dinner table, and Jesus looking over and seeing a vine on the wall. He might have walked over to it and said, "Hey guys, see this vine? (Pretend to hold up a vine.) **The vine is me. The branches** (pretend to reach for the branches) **are you. Apart from me,** (grab an imaginary branch and break it off) **you can do nothing!** (Throw the imaginary branch on the floor then reach for another imaginary branch.) **But stay attached to me, and you can bear a lot of fruit." And then Jesus went on to explain how we bear fruit for him—by loving each other.**

Form groups of six or fewer. Ask each group to use their writing skills to create an act of worship based on the illustration Jesus used. Students can write new words to familiar songs, or create a short skit, poem, or cheer—as long as it illustrates the truth about our need to abide in Christ.

Give groups about ten minutes to create their worship experience. Offer help to any groups having trouble coming up with ideas.

When groups are ready, ask students to take turns sharing what they created as a worship offering to God.

Praise Rap

Scripture: Psalm 100; Ephesians 5:19-20
Theme: Music
Experience: In this **act of praise, music experience,** and **prayer of thanksgiving,** students will proclaim their faith in God using rap songs.
Preparation: You'll need Bibles.

Worship

ather students in a circle. Ask:
- **What kind of music do you like to listen to?**
- **What's your favorite praise song?**
- **How does music make you feel when you listen to it?**
- **How do you think God feels when we praise him?**

Say: **Listen to what the Bible says about praising God.**

Have students form two groups, and give each group a Bible. Have a reader in each group read aloud Psalm 100. Say: **This writer says we should praise God with shouts of joy and singing. Often, the psalms were sung and shouted aloud, sort of like today's rap music. Let's turn this psalm into a proclamation of praise, from us to God.**

Explain that the first group should develop a rap song, with actions, using Psalm 100:1-3. The second group should do the same with verses 4 and 5. Give students ten minutes to develop and practice their raps, then have groups present their songs as praise to God. If desired, let groups teach each other their raps, then have the whole group present the psalm together.

Have students form a circle. Then read aloud Ephesians 5:19-20. Say: **The Bible says it's good for us to praise God with song and thanksgiving. We've already**

praised him with song; now let's praise him with thanksgiving. Begin a prayer of thanksgiving, then go around the circle and let each person add something that he or she is thankful to God for. Then close by singing your group's favorite praise song.

Walk of Thanks

Scripture: Psalm 75:1
Theme: Giving Thanks
Experience: In this **prayer of thanksgiving**, students will use every-
day objects to remind them to thank God.
Preparation: You'll need a Bible.

Worship

ather students in a circle. Read aloud Psalm 75:1. Ask:

- **What are you most thankful to God for?**
- **Why is it important to thank God for all he's given us?**

Say: **Today we're going to do an activity to help us remember to thank God at all times. It's called a Walk of Thanks. It's a lot like the game I Spy that you played when you were little. We'll go for a walk together. As we go, each person will name an object you see, and connect it to a reason to thank God. For example, I might say, "I see the street, which provides a way to go places. I thank God for Jesus, who provides a way for me to go to heaven."**

Lead students outside for a walk around the neighborhood or the church grounds. (If the weather is bad, you can have students walk around the inside of the church building, and name things they see as they go.) As you walk, invite students to take turns naming things they see that remind them of reasons to thank God. If students seem stumped, offer suggestions, such as, "I see the street signs where we receive guidance about how to travel from place to place, and I thank God for the Bible, where he wrote important messages to guide us through life," or "I see the cement which gives the buildings a strong foundation, and I thank God for telling us to build our lives on the foundation of faith."

Let students continue the exercise until everyone has shared at least twice. Close the activity by leading students in a prayer, thanking God for each one of them by name.

The Truth of the Word

Scripture: 2 Timothy 3:16

Theme: Valuing God's Word

Experience: In this **declaration of faith** and **prayer of thanksgiving,** students will express their belief in the authority of the Bible.

Preparation: You'll need a Bible and a Scrabble board game.

Worship

ather students in a circle, and read aloud 2 Timothy 3:16. Ask:

- **Do you believe the Bible is true? Why or why not?**
- **What part of the Bible do you think non-Christians have trouble believing?**

Say: **One part of the Bible that seems to be in dispute with non-Christians is the creation of the universe.**

Ask:

- **What theories, other than God creating the universe, have you heard of?**

Say: **Some people believe in what's called the big-bang theory—that some kind of cosmic accident happened that resulted in our universe.**

Ask:

- **If someone told you that theory, what would you say to convince them of the truth—that God created the universe?**

Say: **Here's a little demonstration to help you visualize the truth of the Bible.** Bring out the Scrabble game, and give each person a small handful of letters. At your signal, have students all toss their letters on a table. Say: **Our universe being formed by an accident is about as believable as these letters we just threw forming a dictionary on their own. God created our universe, just as the Bible says he did. Let's use these letters to form words that show we believe what the Bible says.**

Have each student use the letters on the table to form a word that represents one thing they believe about the Bible. For example, students might use the letters to form the words "Jesus," "heaven," or "salvation." After everyone has formed a word, have students take turns presenting their words and why they chose them.

Then lead a circle prayer in which students each say their word in turn, praising and thanking God for the truths contained in the Bible.

The Light of the World

Scripture: Matthew 5:14-16

Theme: Living for Jesus

Experience: In this **artistic experience** and **act of commitment**, students will try to block the light of a candle, then commit to shining their "light" for Jesus.

Preparation: You'll need a Bible, poster board, tape, scissors, a candle for each person, and matches.

Worship

Turn out the lights in your room. Sit with students in a circle. Light a candle, and read aloud Matthew 5:14-16. Ask:

• **What do you think Jesus means when he says we are the light of the world?**

• **What can you do in your life to be a light for Jesus?**

• **Can the light of Christ become "blocked" in your life? Explain.**

While the lights are still off, set your candle on the floor in a corner of the room. Set out poster board, scissors, and tape. Challenge students to use the supplies to completely block out the light of the candle. Make sure students leave plenty of space between the candle flame and the poster board to avoid any fire danger (two feet or more).

When students complete the task to the best of their ability, gather around the blocked candlelight, and ask:

• **Is it hard to completely block the light from the candle? Why or why not?**

• **How do people hide their lights from view in today's world?**

• **What keeps the light of Jesus from shining clearly in your life?**

Have one or two volunteers take away the poster board so the candle is fully visible. Then ask:

• **What do we have to do to let Jesus' light shine fully through us?**

• **Why is Jesus worthy of our complete surrender and our commitment to let his light shine freely through us?**

Have students pray silently for a minute or two, asking God to help them be lights for those around them. Then give each person a candle. Use the flame from the candle in the corner to light the candle of the person on your left. Then have that person light the next person's candle, and so on around the circle. As each person's candle is lit, have students each say one way they'll try to let Jesus shine through them in the coming week. Students might say they'll pray at lunch at school, invite someone to church, or refrain from gossiping. When everyone's candle is lit, lead the group in singing a favorite praise song.

Hindered Offerings

Scripture: Matthew 5:23-24

Theme: Reconciliation

Experience: In this **offering** and **prayer of intercession**, students will give their grievances against others to God, and offer to serve God this week.

Preparation: You'll need a Bible, paper, pens, newsprint, a marker, and an offering plate.

Worship

Tell students they're going to present an offering to God today as a way to worship him. Then say: **Offerings don't have to be monetary to please God. We can give of our talents and our time, too.** Place a sheet of newsprint on the floor and draw a large circle on it to represent an offering plate. Have students sit on the floor around the newsprint. Then say: **Think of your life as one giant offering plate. You can give each day to God in lots of ways—not just with some money on Sunday mornings. For example, when we sing to God, we're using our talents to give him an offering of praise. Let's give God a praise offering together.**

Lead students in singing a praise song they are familiar with. Halfway through the song, stop suddenly and say: **Wait a minute! I forgot about something that's very important when it comes to worshipping God. Let's read about it together.**

Read aloud Matthew 5:23-24. Ask:

• **What does it mean to be reconciled to someone?**

• **What is this passage saying we should do before we can worship God freely?**

• **Why is it important to be reconciled to someone with whom we're having trouble?**

• **What do you think might happen if we refuse to be reconciled?**

Distribute paper and pens. Say: **Think of someone who you need to be reconciled to. Maybe there's someone in school who you've been arguing with, or maybe you're having a problem with someone in your family. Write that person's name on your piece of paper.**

When the offering plate comes around to you, place your paper in the plate as a way to tell God that you want to be reconciled to the person you've named. Pass an offering plate around the circle, and have students place their papers in the offering plate.

When all of the papers have been collected, say: **To be right with God, Jesus tells us to be right with each other. This week, do your best to be reconciled with the person you named. Pray about what to say to the person, and read your Bible to make sure your heart is on the right path and pleasing to God. Then you can make your offering to God the way the Bible tells us to.**

Ask:

• **People don't leave offerings at the altar anymore. What kinds of offerings to God do we make today?**

After several students have responded, say: **Those are some great answers. One of my favorite ways to worship God is by serving others. The Bible says when we show love to others by serving them, we're showing love and service to God. Think of one thing you can do this week as an offering to God. Maybe you'll offer your time by helping an elderly neighbor with yardwork. Or maybe you'll use your talents at math to help a classmate who's struggling. When the marker comes to you, write how you'll offer yourself to God this week, and then read aloud what you've written.**

Give students a moment to think. Then write inside the newsprint circle something you'll do this week to offer yourself to God, and read it aloud. Then pass the marker around the circle. After each person has written a way to offer himself or herself to God, have students stand and each hold onto a section of the newsprint offering plate. Close by praying: **Dear Lord, please make our whole lives an offering to you. And please help us to be reconciled to one another, so our offerings are pleasing to you. Thank you for your love and forgiveness. Help us to love and forgive each other. In your name, amen.**

Believing in the "Unseen" God

Scripture: John 20:29

Theme: Faith

Experience: In this **creative writing experience** and **declaration of faith**, teenagers will understand what it means to believe in something they haven't seen.

Preparation: You'll need a Bible, poster board, tape, a marker, paper, and pencils. Before the activity, write the following statements on a sheet of poster board and tape it to the wall:

- This is what we believe about friends and telling secrets...
- This is what we believe makes a super sports team...
- This is what we believe would be the best place in the world to live...
- This is what we believe about Jesus' resurrection...

Worship

Form four groups, and give each group paper and pencils. Tell students to work with their group to write one response to each of the four statements on the wall.

After each group has written their responses, have groups take turns sharing their responses to the first three statements. Then ask:

- **Have you ever known a friend who betrays secrets?**
- **Have you ever seen a super sports team?**
- **Have you ever visited a beautiful location and thought about what it would be like to live there?**
- **What has led you to believe these things you wrote—because someone told you or because you have seen or experienced them yourself? Explain.**

Have each group share its response to the fourth statement. After all the groups have shared, ask:

- **Were you present at Jesus' resurrection?**
- **Have you ever seen Jesus personally?**
- **Why do you believe in the resurrection of Jesus if you haven't seen him with your own eyes? Explain.**

Read aloud John 20:29. Say: **Jesus said we are especially blessed because we have chosen to believe that Jesus was resurrected and is living among**

us today through his Spirit—even though none of us witnessed his resurrection with our own eyes. God is pleased with that kind of faith.

As a declaration of their faith in God, have students write out personal faith statements. Provide paper and pencils, and have students divide their papers into three sections. In the first section, have students write what they believe about the "unseen" God. In the second section, have students write what they believe about the "unseen" Jesus. In the third section, have students write what they believe about the "unseen" Holy Spirit.

When students are finished, have them take turns reading their papers as a prayer to God.

The Call to Character

Scripture: Micah 6:8

Theme: Developing Character

Experience: In this **commissioning** and **creative reading** experience, teenagers will learn the importance of developing Christian character.

Preparation: You'll need pencils, and a copy of the "What the Lord Requires" handout (p. 88) for each person.

Worship

This commissioning activity is a great way to prepare students who are headed off to a mission experience, getting ready to serve in a special capacity in the church, or any time you want students to focus on the importance of developing Christian character.

Have students form a circle, and give each person a pencil and a copy of the "What the Lord Requires" handout (p. 88). Have students read through the handout and write a specific example next to each "Youth Response" heading. For example, under the "To act justly" section, a youth response might be "Don't cheat on tests," or "Don't lie to my parents." Tell students they will be sharing their responses with the group.

When students are finished, lead them through the creative reading. Each time you come to a "Youth Response," go around the circle, and have each person share what he or she wrote in that section. Continue until you've led students through the whole reading.

After the reading, have students give themselves a round of applause for their commitment to doing what's right in God's eyes.

Close this experience with a prayer service. As the leader, start the prayer service with the following: **Lord, you provided these young people with a wonderful opportunity to serve you. May they treat justly those they come into contact with. May they give mercy to those who wrong them. And may they, in all situations, walk humbly, giving you the credit for all their successes. Hear each person now as we give ourselves and our ministries to you.**

Go around the circle allowing each person to pray out loud. (Shy students may pass by tapping the shoulder of the person next to them.) Then close the prayer time by saying: **Amen!**

The Ultimate Power Service

Scripture: Exodus 15:1-12

Theme: God's Power

Experience: In this **artistic experience** and **complete service**, teenagers will design creative ways to worship God for his power in their lives.

Preparation: You'll need paper, pencils, worship songbooks and/or CDs of worship music, books of Christian poetry, and assorted art supplies (such as watercolor paints, markers, and drawing paper). Optional: a television, VCR, and a videotape of the movie *Prince of Egypt*, cued to the scene where the Israelites cross the Red Sea.

Worship

If you can, show a video clip from the movie *Prince of Egypt* where the Israelites cross the Red Sea.

After the clip, have the group read Exodus 15:1-12, the song of praise Moses sang after the Red Sea crossing. Then ask:

• **What does this praise song (and video clip) say about God's power?**

• **The Bible repeatedly says that God is all-powerful. What does that mean to you personally?**

• **Why should we praise God for his power in our lives?**

Say: **God is all-powerful. And he has given us the ability to praise him for his power—with music and poetry and art, and many other ways. Today we're going to work together to design a worship presentation for God.**

What the Lord Requires

Leader: What does God require of you?

Youth: To act justly.

Leader: What does it mean to act justly?

Youth Response: _____

Leader: What else does he require?

Youth: To love mercy.

Leader: What does it mean to love mercy?

Youth Response: _____

Leader: What else does he require?

Youth: To walk humbly with our God.

Leader: What does it mean to walk humbly with God?

Youth Response: _____

Leader: He has showed you, O youth, what is good. And what does the Lord require of you? To act justly and to love mercy and to walk humbly with your God.

–(adapted from Micah 6:8)

Form three groups. Tell groups that they will be responsible for creating a unique portion of the worship presentation for God. Have each group choose a different creative way to worship God. For example, one group might choose music, while another chooses poetry, art, or drama. Provide each group with supplies for their chosen mode of expression. Tell groups they can use ideas from the resources you've provided to create their worship presentation; but encourage them to rely mostly on their own imaginations and the song of Moses to come up with an original presentation. Tell groups their finished presentation should last between five and ten minutes.

Once students have their assignment, have them begin creating their presentations. If students have trouble thinking of ideas, offer these suggestions:

• Music—Have students write a new worship song based on Exodus 15:1-12. Encourage them to use the melodies of the worship songs you've provided, or some other song they're all familiar with.

• Poetry—Have students present a creative reading of an original worship they create together, or have them combine favorite quotes from existing poems to create a unique poetry presentation that focuses on God's power.

• Art—Have students design a mural that depicts the many ways God demonstrates his power in our lives.

• Drama—Have students create a skit that illustrates God's awesome power in our lives.

Allow groups plenty of time to work on their creations. When they're finished, have groups take turns presenting their creative worship to God. Close by having students read Exodus 15:1-12 as a prayer to God.

As an option, you might want to have students present their worship creations to the whole church in an upcoming service.

Communion in Common Places

Scripture: Luke 22:14-20

Theme: Living for Jesus

Experience: In this **celebration of the Lord's supper** and **declaration of faith**, students will participate in the Lord's Supper in a public setting.

Preparation: You'll need index cards, pencils, a basket, and a loaf of bread and a bottle of grape juice for every fifteen students. You'll also need to provide transportation. You will need to have an authorized person lead the Lord's Supper service.

Worship

nce everyone has arrived, read Luke 22:14-20. Then say: **When Jesus and his disciples joined in the first Lord's Supper, they were in a private location, away from the public. Today we're going to join in celebrating the Lord's Supper together—but with a twist. We're going to do it in a public place as a declaration of our faith in Jesus.**

Load students into cars (or a van or bus) and drive them to a place they often hang out, such as a mall food court, public property in front of a school, or a park. When you arrive, have students gather together.

Say: **Today we're going to have our own special Lord's Supper service. On the night Jesus was betrayed he was having the Passover dinner with his disciples. While they were eating, he took some bread and he said "This is my body given for you; do this in remembrance of me." Likewise he took some wine and said, "This cup is the new covenant in my blood, which is poured out for you." And then he told the disciples that as often as they drink from the cup and break the bread, they would be reminded of the sacrifice of Christ on the cross until he came again.**

At this point take the bread, hold it up and say: **This is symbolic of Christ's body in our world. If we sit at the table with him, we cannot also sit at the table with sin. By sharing this, let's agree to share our table only with Christ every day, no matter where we are or what we are doing.** Pass the bread around the circle.

Next take the juice out and hold it up and say: **This is symbolic of Christ's blood in our world. Let's share this in remembrance of him, remembering that he wants to be in control of our lives, wherever we go.** Pass the juice around the circle.

After the Lord's Supper, ask:

• **How does it feel to remember Christ through this service in this "everyday place"?**

• **Why is it important to remember Christ in this place we have chosen?**

• **Are there places you go where Jesus would not be welcome to join you?**

Give each person an index card and a pencil, then have them write their response to your last question. Lead students in prayer, dedicating the school, mall, park or other place to God's glory. Then pass around a basket. Invite students to place their cards in the basket as a demonstration of their willingness to invite Jesus to go with them everywhere they go in life. Close with this prayer: **Father, we all have those dark places in our lives where we go and we leave you out. We give you now those places where you have never before been invited and we ask that you will come and sit with us and be our Lord in all the places of our lives. In Jesus' name we pray. Amen.**

Bonfire Thanksgiving

Scripture: Psalm 54:6-7
Theme: Giving Thanks
Experience: In this **prayer of thanksgiving**, students will symbolically lift their praise to God around a bonfire.
Preparation: You'll need an outdoor location and a bonfire. You'll also need index cards and pencils. This activity works well around Thanksgiving.

Worship

Once everyone has arrived at the bonfire, give every person two index cards and a pencil. Tell students that during the course of the evening, the bonfire is going to be a thanksgiving altar where we can bring our praise and gratitude to God.

Lead students in singing three or four worship songs. After the songs, read aloud Psalm 54:6-7. Then, on one index card, have students write an answer to this question:

• **What's the best thing that God has done for you this year that you are most thankful for?**

When students finish, ask several volunteers to share what they have written to question 1. Then lead students in another praise chorus. As they sing, have students throw their praises into the fire, symbolically offering their thanks up to God.

On the second card, have students write a response to this question:

• **What's the hardest thing you have found to give thanks for this year?**

When students finish, ask several volunteers to share what they have written to question 2. Then lead students in another praise chorus. As they sing, have students throw their praises into the fire, symbolically offering their thanks up to God—even for the difficult things that have happened.

Close by reading Psalm 54:6-7 again, and encourage students to be thankful in all things in the coming year.

The Prodigal's Return

Scripture: Luke 15

Theme: God's Forgiveness

Experience: In this **creative writing experience, artistic experience,** and **sharing time,** teenagers will think about how God welcomes us back even after we really mess up.

Preparation: You'll need a Bible, paper, markers, a stack of old magazines, several pairs of scissors, and glue.

Worship

Read Luke 15:1-10 aloud. Ask:

- **Have you ever lost something extremely valuable?**
- **How did you attempt to locate it?**

Distribute paper and markers. Say: **Jesus told these parables so that we might understand how valuable we are to God and how he longs for our return when we stray from him.** On their papers, have students create a simple self-portrait, and surround it with personal details that might be included on a "Lost" or "Wanted" poster.

As teenagers are finishing their drawings, ask:

- **Can you share a time when you strayed from God?**

Say: **The remaining verses in this chapter tell a similar story.** Read Luke 15:11-32 aloud. Ask:

- **How does the father in this parable resemble God?**
- **How do we sometimes resemble the older son in this passage? the younger son?**

Say: **The younger son felt he was such a disappointment to his father. While he wanted to return home, he worried that he had messed up too badly to be forgiven.**

Ask:

• **Have you ever been worried that God might not forgive you, or felt too embarrassed to ask for his forgiveness? Explain.**

Distribute sheets of paper, scissors, glue and magazines to students. Say: **Use these supplies to create a storyboard, based on your experiences, that has a plot similar to the parable we have just studied. Cut pictures from the magazines provided to illustrate your story.**

When everyone has finished, allow time for volunteers to share their story. Spend time together thanking God for giving us so many second chances.

Filling Life With God

Scripture: Romans 12:9-21

Theme: Holy Living

Experience: In this artistic experience and sharing time, teenagers will evaluate their character and think about the way God wants us to live.

Preparation: For this outdoor activity, you'll need a sizable paved area, enough sidewalk chalk for each participant, and a Bible. If you prefer to lead this activity indoors, cover the floor with newsprint, and use crayons in place of chalk.

Worship

Distribute sidewalk chalk to each teenager. Direct kids to work together to outline their bodies onto the pavement, writing their names beneath their drawings. Read Romans 12:9-21 aloud. Say: **Each day we make decisions about how we treat each other.**

Ask:

• **What are some of the qualities God wants us to pursue?**

• **What can we do to develop these virtues?**

Say: **There are several qualities and behaviors listed in this passage that should mark our lives as Christians. Using your chalk, take a moment to fill in one another's chalk outlines with the qualities you appreciate about that person.** Help teenagers get started by writing encouraging comments in several of the drawings. As kids write, make sure no one is left out by encouraging kids to write something positive inside each chalk outline.

After a time of sharing and affirmation, discuss the qualities and attributes of God reflected in the Bible passage you read earlier. Ask:

• **What characteristics do you most appreciate about God?**

• **How can we learn to be more like God in our character and behavior toward others?**

Create another simple chalk outline on the pavement and label it "God." Have kids write inside the outline qualities and actions they appreciate about God.

When they finish, have kids gather around the God outline, and review what everyone wrote. Close with prayer, thanking God for his goodness and asking for his help in our pursuit to become more like him in our character and behavior.

Holy Offerings

Scripture: Psalm 51:16-17

Theme: Giving to God

Experience: In this **offering** and **act of commitment**, kids will evaluate what God desires of us.

Preparation: You'll need several wrapped boxes containing simple gifts that a teenager wouldn't enjoy at all—for example, staples, a can opener, a CD of elevator music, or a package of napkins. You'll also need a Bible, poster board, markers, index cards, gift wrap, tape, and scissors.

Worship

Distribute wrapped gifts to several students. As the gifts are opened, explain that at some point we have probably all received (or given) the "you really shouldn't have" gift. Sometimes we just don't really know what a person likes. Ask:

• **Can you think of some examples of gifts you have received that you didn't want or haven't really enjoyed?**

Read Psalm 51:16-17 aloud. Say: **Sometimes we offer God gifts that are totally inappropriate. He must think, "You don't really know what I like, do you?"**

Ask:

• **Can you think of a time when you suffered unnecessarily with guilt, or did something unnecessary because you thought it would somehow** please God? Explain.

• **Can you remember an incident when you did something nice, but had completely wrong motives for doing it? Explain.**

• **How does pride or self-importance sometimes get in the way of true worship?**

Write "God's Wish List" at the top of a sheet of poster board. Distribute markers and ask teenagers to write on the poster board gifts that God might ask for. Remind them of Psalm 51:16-17 as they begin.

As they finish, distribute index cards. Have kids each write a prayer of commitment to God, offering him things he might desire of them. Have kids wrap their cards in wrapping paper, and place them in a pile below the poster board.

Close by having kids take turns praying, offering their gifts to God. After the prayer, encourage kids to take their wrapped index cards home as a reminder to fulfill their commitment to God.

What God Wills

Scripture: James 1:27

Theme: God's Will

Experience: In this **service opportunity**, students will act upon the Scripture they study.

Preparation: You'll need several flashlights, stationery, pens, and the names and addresses of several elderly members of your congregation. Optional: an adult volunteer dressed up like Bigfoot.

Worship

As students enter the darkened church or youth room, distribute flashlights at the door and explain their mission—to find the elusive Bigfoot. Form teams and send kids around the church grounds. If possible, have an adult volunteer dress up like Bigfoot and peek at kids around corners from time to time, being careful not to allow kids to catch him.

After several minutes, call everyone back together and ask:

• **Did you have any luck?**

• **What's frustrating about looking for some fanciful creature like Bigfoot?**

Say: **Sometimes God's will is like the widely rumored Abominable**

Snowman. We suspect it is out there but can't seem to catch it.

Ask:

• **What do you know about God's will for your life?**

Read James 1:27 aloud and ask:

• **Does this give you ideas of things you can do right now to please God?**

• **What can we do as a group to accomplish God's will?**

Say: **Obeying God's will is one of the most important ways we can honor and worship him. And one sure way we can follow God's will, according to James 1:27, is to care for "orphans and widows" in our community. Let's do that today by writing notes of encouragement to some of the elderly folks in our own congregation.**

Distribute stationery and pens. Assign each person an elderly church member to encourage. It's OK if more than one student is assigned the same elderly person. On the stationery, have teenagers write short letters to encourage the elderly in your congregation. If kids wonder what to write, encourage them to tell a little about themselves, and that they're thinking about and praying for their elderly person.

As students are finishing up, ask:

• **What are some good motives for serving others?**

• **What are some bad motives for serving others?**

• **What's the best motivation for doing God's will?**

Give each person one more sheet of stationery. Close by having kids create short written prayers to God. In their letters, encourage kids to express their commitment to serve others in response to God's love and mercy toward them.

Carrying Thanks Around

Scripture: Matthew 26:26-29

Theme: Giving Thanks

Experience: During this **celebration of the Lord's supper** and **prayer of thanksgiving**, students will be reminded of something incredible God has done for them.

Preparation: You'll need bread and grape juice set up in one corner of the room. You'll also need index cards, scissors, a hole punch, string, pens, a CD player, and a CD of worship music. You may also want to ask your pastor or another authorized person to be available to administer the Lord's Supper elements.

Before the activity, cut index cards in half (one-half card for every person). Punch two holes along one edge of each card. Cut 18-inch pieces of string, one for each card. Insert the string through the holes on the cards, and tie in loose bows. Make one of these cards for each person.

Worship

Read Matthew 26:26-29 aloud. Say: **Jesus instituted the Lord's Supper so we would always have a way of remembering that he died for our sins.**
Ask:

• **What other things remind you of God's generosity toward us?**

• **How can we demonstrate gratitude toward God?**

Give each student a pen, and a card with string. Encourage students to find a quiet place in the room where they can pray alone. Say: **Think about the many things God has done for you. Choose the one you feel is most important, and thank him for it. Then write it on the card I gave you.**

While kids are praying, play soft worship music. Invite kids to partake of the Lord's Supper at any time during their prayer. (If your pastor is administering the Lord's Supper elements, have him or her offer the elements to each student in turn.)

After the prayer time and Lord's Supper, invite kids to share what they wrote on their cards. Before closing with prayer, suggest that teenagers wear their cards around their necks throughout the coming week as an expression of their praise and gratitude to God.

Fun Worship With Psalms

Scripture: Psalm 95:1-7

Theme: Praising God

Experience: In this **creative movement, music experience,** and **prayer of thanksgiving,** teenagers will create a worship experience to the words of the psalm.

Preparation: You'll need Bibles, crepe paper, and black markers. Before the experience, cut or tear the crepe paper into 6-foot lengths.

Worship

Say: **Today we're going to prepare a worship experience to praise and thank God for all the blessings in our lives. First, let's share some of our blessings.**

Start off by sharing one blessing in your life, and have kids take turns sharing their blessings. After each blessing, encourage kids to say "praise God" or "thank you, Jesus." Once everyone has shared, distribute crepe paper streamers and black markers. Tell kids to each write their own blessing on the streamer, as one word or several words.

Then have kids break into two groups: musicians and dancers. Instruct groups to plan how to illustrate Psalm 95:1-7 in music or movement. Give groups ten to fifteen minutes of planning time. During that time, ask some of the musicians to act as the rhythm section for worship by finding items they can use as drums. For example, chairs, books, and even knees work well. Encourage the rest of the musicians to create a melody to go along with the words of the psalm. It's OK if kids have to alter the words slightly to match the melody they create, but encourage them to stay as true to the text as possible. Ask the dancers to design some kind of creative movement to go along with the psalm. Encourage everyone to use their "blessing" streamers as part of the worship experience and to illustrate the beautiful words of the psalm in movement and music.

When everyone is ready, invite the groups to perform simultaneously. Repeat your performance, if desired, by changing roles. After the worship experience, gather everyone together and ask:

- **How did it make you feel to worship God like this?**
- **Why does God deserve our worship and praise?**
- **What are some other ways we can worship and thank God for all he has blessed us with?**

Challenge kids to practice worshipping God in creative ways during the coming week.

Love in Action

Scripture: 1 John 4:11-12
Theme: Loving Others

Experience: In this **act of commitment** and **artistic experience,** teenagers will share love with words, actions, and art.

Preparation: You'll need a Bible, paper, scissors, colored markers, and tape.

Worship

ather everyone together and say: **Listen to these words about love from 1 John 4:11-12.** Read aloud the Scripture. Then ask:

• **Why does God want us to love each other?**

• **Should love be conditional or selective? Why or why not?**

• **How should you treat someone who really is not a very nice person?**

• **How can loving others make you a better Christian?**

Say: **Let's explore some different ways to show love. Everybody, up on your feet. First, let's show love with words. Share your love for your fellow classmates with sincere words of kindness, encouragement, friendship, and Christian love.** Have teenagers take a few minutes to circulate in the room and speak words of love to everyone. Have them sit down and ask:

• **What did someone say to you that made you feel really good?**

Then say: **Stand up again, and this time we'll show love without words.** Encourage kids by sharing a hug, a handshake, or a pat on the back with teenagers as they do the same. Then ask:

• **How did someone make you feel loved without words?**

Say: **Now let's draw love. Draw a way that you can commit to showing love to another person to make God's love complete in you. Draw a loving act you plan to do for a family member, friend, acquaintance, or even a stranger.**

Distribute paper, colored markers, and scissors, and show kids how to cut linking hearts. Use the illustration below as a guide. Have kids draw pictures on the hearts of a loving act they will commit to, then decorate the room with the

hearts by taping them to the walls. As each person tapes up his or her picture, have kids share their commitments to show love to another person. Close by reading 1 John 4:11-12 again, and say: **Loving others is one of the most important ways we can worship God. Thanks for worshipping God with me today.**

Cross Confessions

Scripture: Hebrews 9:28; 10:19-23

Theme: Easter

Experience: In this **artistic experience** and **prayer of confession**, teenagers will offer their sins to Jesus to ask his forgiveness and recognize his great sacrifice.

Preparation: You'll need Bibles, twigs, string, scissors, modeling clay or small plastic foam blocks, slips of colored paper, pens, and sandwich bags (fold-over type).

Worship

ay: **Easter season is a time to contemplate the greatest sacrifice of all—the gift that God gave of his only Son, who died for our sins so that we might have eternal life with him in heaven. Today we're going to share a worship experience as we ask forgiveness for our sins and praise God for his great gift.**

Have twigs, string, scissors, and modeling clay or small plastic foam blocks set out, and instruct teenagers to make crosses of the twigs and string, and stand them up in the clay or blocks. When everyone is finished, line up the crosses on a table in the front of the room.

Next distribute small pieces of colored paper, pens, string, and sandwich bags.

Say: **God promises forgiveness for our sins through our faith in him. Take a few minutes to privately write on these slips of paper some sins you need forgiveness for. Fold the papers, drop them in the bags, and tie them shut with a string. Leave a few extra inches of string on your bags.**

When everyone is finished, ask for four volunteer readers to read Hebrews 9:28; 10:19-23. After the Scripture is read, send teenagers up to the table to tie their bags of sins to their crosses. After the last person is finished, ask students to join you as you pray aloud a prayer of confession of your own or one similar to the following prayer: **Heavenly Father, you sent your only Son to die for our sins so that we might live forever with you. We are truly sorry and beg your forgiveness for the wrong things we do. We ask for your guidance as we try to live good lives and love one another as you have taught us to do. Bless us with wisdom and strength to avoid temptation so we can be the best that we can be. Amen.**

Have kids take their crosses home as a reminder to ask God to forgive their weaknesses and make them strong.

All Things Are Possible

Scripture: Philippians 4:13
Theme: Perseverance
Experience: In this **declaration of faith**, teenagers will share their goals and find strength in Christ to one day achieve them.
Preparation: You'll need a Bible.

Worship

ave teenagers sit in a circle. Say: **Take a minute to think of something you want to accomplish in your life. It might seem difficult or even impossible right now, but it should be a goal or dream that you have.**

After a minute or two, have everyone listen as you read Philippians 4:13.

Then have teenagers stand up one at a time to shout out their dream or goal. As each person stands up, he or she should take the hand of the person next to him or her, so everyone has joined hands by the time the whole circle is standing. Lead the group in raising their hands high together and shouting, **"I can do everything through him who gives me strength!"**

Sit down again and ask:

• **How can your faith make you stronger?**

• **How might your faith in God help you achieve this goal?**

• **What can you do if your goal seems so impossible that you will never achieve it?**

Stand up, join hands again, and ask: **Is there anything you can't do?** Then have kids raise their hands together as everyone shouts: **I can do everything through him who gives me strength! Praise the Lord!**

The God of Miracles

Scripture: Psalm 77:14

Theme: Faith

Experience: In this **creative reading** and **prayer of intercession**, teenagers will review some of God's miracles, and then pray for a miracle.

Preparation: You'll need a Bible, and a copy of the "Jesus, Worker of Miracles!" handout (pp. 103-104) for each person.

Worship

Read Psalm 77:14. Ask,

• **What is your initial reaction to God being a miracle-working God?**

• **Tell of a miracle that has occurred in your life or the life of someone you know (or the closest thing to a miracle).**

• **What do miracles tell us about God? his power?**

Distribute a copy of the "Jesus, Worker of Miracles!" handout (pp. 103-104) to each person, and ask for volunteers for the five Reader parts. Have each Reader stand to read his or her part. Then lead kids through the creative reading. After the reading, ask:

• **Why do you think having faith was so important to Jesus when he performed miracles?**

• **How can you show your faith in God?**

• **Have you seen evidence of miracles in your life? Explain.**

Say: **Let's think of a miracle that we can pray for together.** Take a few minutes to discuss something you would like to pray for as a prayer of intercession that would take a "miracle" to happen. Open with a short prayer, then ask anyone who would like to add to the prayer to speak aloud or pray silently. Close with everyone saying together: **Praise God, worker of miracles!**

Preparing for Christ's Return

Scripture: 1 Thessalonians 4:13-18

Theme: Second Coming of Christ

Experience: In this **meditation**, kids will be challenged to prepare themselves for the return of Christ.

Jesus, Worker of Miracles!

Reader 1: A furious storm rose as Jesus and his disciples were crossing the lake in a boat. Jesus slept as the waves swept over the boat, and his disciples shouted for Jesus to save them. He replied, "You of little faith, why are you so afraid?" He calmed the winds and the waves, and his men were amazed. They asked, "What kind of man is this? Even the winds and the waves obey him."

All: Praise God, worker of miracles!

Reader 2: As Jesus was teaching one day, some men came carrying their paralyzed friend on a mat. When they could not get through the crowd to see Jesus, they went up on the roof and lowered him through the crowd, right in front of Jesus. When Jesus saw their faith, he said, "Friend, your sins are forgiven…I tell you, get up, take your mat and go home." The man stood up and went home praising God. The people said, "We have seen remarkable things today."

All: You are the God who performs miracles; you display your power among the peoples.

Reader 3: A large crowd of five thousand gathered as Jesus was preaching, and he asked his disciples where to buy bread so all these people could eat. Andrew responded, "Here is a boy with five small barley loaves and two small fish, but how far will they go among so many?" But Jesus knew what he would do. He had the crowd sit down, gave thanks for the food, and distributed the food so everyone had as much as he or she could eat. When the disciples gathered the leftovers, they filled twelve baskets with pieces of the barley loaves. When the people saw the miracle, they said, "Surely this is the prophet who is to come into the world."

All: Praise God, worker of miracles!

Reader 4: Two blind men followed Jesus down the street, calling out, "Have mercy on us, Son of David!" Jesus asked them, "Do you believe that I am able to do this?" "Yes, Lord," they replied. He touched their eyes and said, "According to your faith will it be done to you," and he restored their sight.

All: You are the God who performs miracles; you display your power among the peoples.

Reader 5: Jesus' friend Lazarus lay sick, so his sisters, Mary and Martha, sent word for Jesus to come. But when Jesus arrived, Lazarus was dead. He asked to see the tomb and then ordered the stone removed. Martha protested since Lazarus had already been dead four days. But Jesus said, "Did I not tell you that if you believed, you would see the glory of God?" Jesus called, "Lazarus, come out!" and Lazarus walked out of the tomb, still wrapped in the burial linen.

All: Praise God, worker of miracles! Oh Lord, who has power to calm nature, heal the sick, and raise the dead, we believe in your power and have faith that you will save us. Amen.

Preparation: You'll need to recruit one young teen as a volunteer actor before this experience. Inform the volunteer that he or she will be trying to convince the rest of the class that Christ has returned and they have all been left behind.

Worship

Instruct six young people to leave the room under the pretense of finding some things you need for this activity. One of the young people leaving should be the volunteer. The volunteer will take the others to another room and fill them in on what is about to take place. While this is going on, tell the ones remaining in the room with you that you forgot to tell the six something, then leave the room. As soon as you are with the six, have the volunteer actor return to the main meeting room very excited and frightened. Tell the actor to try to convince the others that the rest of you have suddenly disappeared. After the volunteer has had a few seconds to convince the others that Jesus has returned and they have all been left behind, have everyone return to the main meeting room.

Don't be surprised if many of the young people are not convinced. Those who are strong in their faith should be the hardest to convince. The object of the activity is to get the students thinking about the second coming of Christ and their own preparedness for that event.

Discuss the group's reaction to the volunteer by asking:

• **Did you believe the actor? Why or why not?**

• **Do you ever think about the second coming of Christ? Why or why not?**

• **How do you think it would feel to be left behind when Christ comes again to call us to be with him?**

• **What can we do now to prepare ourselves for Christ's coming?**

Allow a few to share their experiences. Read 1 Thessalonians 4:13-18. Ask for volunteers to briefly describe the events that they think will take place when Jesus returns. Then instruct your group to sit quietly with their eyes shut and imagine the events you are about to relate.

Say: **Close your eyes and imagine with me for a moment. There's the sound of a trumpet coming from the heavens, and a shout of the archangel that is heard around the world. You look toward the sky and see Jesus descending on the clouds. At that same instant, graves begin to open and people rise up from them. Immediately, you begin to feel yourself change and rise in** the air too. You are going to meet Jesus.

Right now, with your eyes still closed, tell Jesus how thankful you are that he has welcomed you into his family of believers. Ask him to show you how you can prepare yourself for his return.

At this time of guided worship, instruct your group to open their eyes, join hands and form a circle. Say: **Not everyone will join Jesus in the air. Those left behind are those who have never accepted Jesus' death as payment for their own sin. If you feel like God is speaking to you, asking you to accept Jesus' death as payment for your sin, I am giving you an opportunity to do that now. Everyone bow your head. If you want to accept Jesus' death as your payment, then right now tell God. Tell him you know you will die for your sin without Jesus but you don't want to do that. Tell him you accept Jesus' death as payment for your sin and want to be his child. Thank him for promising to accept Jesus' death for your payment.**

For you who are Christians, think of your friends and family who would be left behind if Jesus did return today. Ask God to put a greater desire in your heart to tell them about Jesus.

After giving the group a minute to pray in silence, close the time with your own prayer of commitment to follow Jesus.

After the prayer, ask any who made a decision to accept Jesus' death as payment for their sin to tell an adult. Encourage kids to ask any questions they might have about what it means to be a Christian.

The Foundation of the Church

Scripture: 1 Corinthians 3:9-11

Theme: Jesus' Importance

Experience: In this **artistic experience** and **prayer of thanksgiving**, young people will recognize Jesus as the only foundation for the church and for their own lives.

Preparation: You'll need index cards, pencils, and tape.

Worship

Form groups of three or four, and give each group pencils, tape, and a stack of index cards.

Say: **Your group's task is to build a church using the index**

cards and tape. But before you can begin construction, you must build the right foundation.

Ask kids to call out things that they think might form the "foundation" of the church. Make sure kids understand that you're not talking about physical materials such as lumber and nails, but spiritual materials. Some possible responses include the spiritual fruit of love, joy, or peace, or more tangible things like the Bible, pastors, or Christians. Give volunteers a chance to share why they think these things might form the foundation of the church. As kids call out items, have groups write each response on a separate index card.

Then say: **The cards on the bottom of your church's foundation are the most important because they hold up all the others. To find out what the foundation of the church really is, read 1 Corinthians 3:9-11 in your Bibles.**

After groups read the Scripture, ask:

• **Why does the Bible say that Jesus is the foundation of the church?**

Say: **Jesus is the only true foundation for the church because without him, nothing else can stand. Without Jesus, there is no love, no peace, and no salvation. Without him, there are no Christians, no pastors, and no Christian youth groups.**

Have group members write "Jesus" on four separate index cards. Then say: Use these cards to form the foundation of your church. Then use the other pieces you have to create the rest of the structure.

Give groups about five minutes to complete their churches. Then ask:

• **What did you learn about the church through this experience?**

• **What did you learn about Jesus?**

• **How are we "God's building"?**

• **Based on what you've learned in this experience, why should we worship Jesus?**

Say: **The church is made up of all people who believe Jesus is the Son of God and died as payment for our sins. Everything in the church—and in our lives as individual Christians—rests and relies on Jesus. For this reason we should always be humble toward Christ, and praise him for his goodness toward us.**

Have groups gather around their church creations and join hands. Lead kids in singing a song of praise to Jesus. Close the worship time by thanking Jesus for being the foundation of the church, and of our lives.

God First

Scripture: Genesis 22:1-18

Theme: Putting God First

Experience: In this **act of commitment**, teenagers will decide whether they're willing to give up an "idol" in their lives.

Preparation: You'll need Bibles, index cards, pens, construction paper, glue, colored pens, and assorted objects such as cotton balls, yarn, buttons, cloth, and magazines.

Worship

sk for several volunteers to take turns reading successive parts of Genesis 22:1-9. Then distribute index cards and pens. On their cards, have kids write their response to this question:

• **What do you want more than anything?**

When kids finish, ask for a few volunteers to share what they wrote. Then ask the whole group:

• **If God asked you to give up what you wrote on your card for his sake, could you? Why or why not?**

• **Why do you think God would ever ask you to give up anything you want?**

Say: **God always wants what's best for us. Because of this, he doesn't want us to value anything more than we value him. Whenever we love something more than we love God, we are making it our object of worship. But God is the only one we should worship.**

Have kids use the supplies you gathered to create a symbol that represents what they wrote on their cards. For example, kids might make a football to symbolize their desire to play football, or a guitar to represent the desire to play guitar.

When kids finish, have them take turns explaining their symbols to the class, and telling why their object or dream is important to them. Then ask:

• **How would you feel if God asked you to give up your item? Explain.**

• **If God did ask you to give it up, could he replace it with something better? Why or why not?**

• **God always wants what's best for us. So if he asked you to give up your item, could you? Why or why not?**

Say: **If you believe you could give up your item for God, I'd like you to toss your card on the floor in front of you.**

Then ask:

• **Why is this an act of worship?**

Say: **Because God loves us and knows what's best for us, he wants us to keep him first in our lives. Our willingness to give up anything for God shows that we worship him above all.**

Ask a volunteer to read the rest of the passage, Genesis 22:10-18. Then say: **God may ask you to give up something meaningful, but then he may give it back. In this situation with Abraham, God not only gave him his son back but made him the "father" of all the Jewish people. When we worship God first in our lives, God gives us all that we need and more.**

Pleasing Aromas

Scripture: Revelation 5:8; 8:3-5

Theme: Prayer

Experience: In this creative **prayer of intercession**, teenagers will make incense to show the way our prayers reach God.

Preparation: You'll need Bibles, a camping stove with fuel, matches, a saucepan, water, pancake syrup, salt, cinnamon, clove, basil, and other assorted fragrant spices. Before the activity, combine 1 cup of water and ½ cup of syrup in a saucepan. Set up the camping stove, and place the saucepan on the burner.

Worship

egin by asking:

• **What do you think is happening in heaven right now?**

• **What sights and sounds do you think people in heaven experience?**

• **What kinds of pleasant aromas do they smell?**

Have a student read Revelation 5:8 and another student read Revelation 8:3-5. Say: **Incense is a symbol that represents our prayers to God. Heaven is filled with our prayers. They rise to God like a pleasant aroma. We're going to worship God today by creating a pleasant aroma for him to enjoy.**

Form groups of three and have each group select one or more spices that they like. In their trios, have kids take turns sharing prayer requests for people they know who have specific needs. For example, maybe they have a friend who is ill, or a non-Christian friend who needs to receive Christ. Once trios have shared their requests, turn on the burner to begin heating the water and syrup mixture. Then say: **In a moment, I'd like you to pray together for the requests you mentioned. After each person in your group prays, I'd like that person to come forward and add a spice to the saucepan. Then return to your trio and let the next person pray. We'll continue until everyone has prayed and added some spice to our pan.**

Have trios pray. As each person comes forward after he or she prays, have him or her add about ½ teaspoon of spice to the saucepan. Keep the flame low so that the mixture simmers but doesn't boil. As kids' prayers (and spices) are added, the room will begin to fill with the aroma of the spices. After all the kids have prayed, invite the whole group to gather around the saucepan and smell the aroma. Then ask:

- **Now that we've prayed, what do you think is happening in heaven?**
- **Why does praying for others please God?**
- **How does God want our hearts to be when we are praying?**
- **How is praying for others a way to worship God?**

Have kids join hands around the saucepan and pray together, thanking God for hearing their prayers and allowing them to worship him by praying for others.

Where He Leads I'll Go

Scripture: Nehemiah 6:5-9

Theme: Trusting God

Experience: In this **act of praise** and **prayer of petition**, teenagers will worship God by committing to trust him more.

Preparation: You'll need several plastic dropcloths (the kind used for painting), enough to cover a 10x20-foot area. You'll also need a dozen eggs, and one blindfold for every two people. Before the activity, cover the floor with the dropcloth.

Worship

A sk a volunteer to read aloud Nehemiah 6:9.

Say: **Jerusalem had been invaded. The walls were broken down and the gates were burned** (Nehemiah 1:3). **This made the people** living there vulnerable to attack. **A long time after the attack, people who had fled the invasion began to return to Jerusalem. They lived in the ruins, getting by as best they could. Nehemiah cared about the condition of the city, and the people who lived there. He knew the people were in danger because their neighbors looked down on them.**

So Nehemiah decided to return to Jerusalem and help his people—by rebuilding the city walls and gates. However, he ran into all kinds of problems. One of his biggest problems was dealing with the people living in the lands surrounding Jerusalem. They didn't want to see the Jewish people succeed in rebuilding their city. So they sent many messages to Nehemiah to trick him into meeting them so that they could harm him. They spread rumors about him and lied to him. They were continually trying to intimidate him and make him give up.

Pause and ask the group the following questions. After they respond to each question, gently place two or three eggs in random places on the plastic dropcloth. After kids respond to all five questions, you should have all twelve eggs set out. Ask:

• **Have you ever been in a situation where someone has tried to intimidate you? Explain.**

• **Have you ever had people spread rumors about you? Explain.**

• **What have you done in response when people treated you this way?**

Say: **Nehemiah is a great role model to us of how to worship God even when bad things happen.** Read aloud Nehemiah 6:5-9. Say: **Nehemiah's prayer is simple and to the point. In the midst of his enemies trying to hurt him he could have turned away from God, but he didn't. Instead, he worshipped God by trusting him to guide him through the dangers he faced.**

Ask:

• **Why is trust a form of worshipping God, especially when bad things happen?**

• **Do you always put your trust in God when tough times come? Why or why not?**

• **If you don't put your trust in God when difficult problems come, what do you do instead?**

• **Who or what are we worshipping when we choose to put our trust in something other than God? Explain.**

Say: **Bad things happen to everyone. But when we put our trust in God, we demonstrate our faith and our willingness to honor God no matter what happens. In return, he guides us through the dangers we encounter in life.**

Point to the eggs on the floor and say: **This egg-laden obstacle course provides us with a picture of the way life can be. Sometimes we feel like blindfolded travelers, trying to make it through life avoiding the many dangers that cross our path. Walking alone, we don't know where to step, and so we often run into "land mines." But by putting our trust in God and worshipping only him, he becomes our guide and gives us strength and direction to navigate safely through the dangers we face. Let's thank God for his guidance and demonstrate our trust in him.**

Have kids form pairs, and give each pair a blindfold. Have both partners remove their shoes. Then have one person in each pair don the blindfold. Tell kids they're going to demonstrate God's trustworthiness by singing worship songs to God while safely guiding their partners through the obstacle course without stepping on any "land mines."

Begin leading kids to sing several worship songs they're familiar with. As they continue to sing to God, have kids go through the obstacle course—one pair at a time. As pairs walk through the obstacle course, have the seeing partner act as a guide for the blindfolded partner. Then have kids switch roles and go through the course again. Continue singing until all the pairs have passed through the obstacle course twice.

After the experience, ask:

• **How did this experience make you feel? Explain.**

• **How is trusting your partner in this experience like trusting God in real life?**

• **How is trusting God a way of worshipping him?**

• **In what areas of your life do you still struggle with trusting God?**

Tell kids they now have an opportunity to practice praying like Nehemiah did. In their pairs, ask kids to share a difficult problem or circumstance they're facing right now. Then have pairs pray together, and ask God for strength and protection in their lives. Encourage students to worship God together by thanking him for the ways they have learned to trust him.

The Names of God

Scripture: Jeremiah 10:6-7

Theme: God's Names

Experience: In this **drama presentation** and **prayer of invocation,** teenagers will learn how to worship God using his names.

Preparation: You'll need a Bible, poster board, markers, and several copies of the "God's Names" handout (p. 115).

Worship

On a sheet of poster board, list several funny first names that aren't used much anymore—for example, Ethel, Bunny, Barney, Rocky, Mildred, and Gomer. Then ask kids to describe what kind of person they think goes best with each name. For example, what does a "Herman" look like? What kind of clothes does he wear? What's his personality like? Write kids' responses next to each name.

Then say: **A name is more than just a label for a person. Names can evoke specific emotions and pictures in us. Our names represent who we are and may sometimes reveal things about our character. For example, a person named "Stone" or "Hunter" might have received that name because of character traits his parents have tried to instill in him.**

Have a volunteer read aloud Jeremiah 10:6-7. Ask:

• **Why do you think the name of God is great and powerful?**

• **What does God's name tell us about his character?**

Say: **Actually, God has many names. Each name represents a different aspect of his character. We can use God's names to worship him.**

Form groups of three or four, and give each group a copy of the "God's Names" handout (p. 115). Read through the list of names and their meanings with kids. Then secretly assign each group one of God's names to explore.

Tell groups that they have ten minutes to prepare a skit that depicts their assigned name of God. Tell kids their skits must tell a story that demonstrates the meaning of their assigned name without ever actually using the name directly. For example, kids can't use the name Prince of Peace in their skit, but they can tell a story of how God brought peace to someone who was troubled. Encourage kids to use their creativity, and to present their skits as an act of worship to God.

When groups are ready, have them take turns presenting their skits. After each skit, have the rest of the class try to guess which name of God the skit was about. Allow kids to use the handout as a hint sheet. Continue until all of the skits have been presented.

Close by having kids join hands for a time of prayer and praise. Have kids each think of one of the names for God that's most meaningful to them. Then close the worship time by going around the circle and having each person worship God by saying the name he or she chose. Once you've gone all the way around the circle, say: **Amen!**

The Potter and the Clay

Scripture: Isaiah 45:9-12

Theme: Acceptance

Experience: In this **artistic experience** and **act of praise**, teenagers will be reminded to worship God by acknowledging him as their creator.

Preparation: You'll need paper, pens, and newsprint. You'll also need modeling clay. If you have time, you can make the clay yourself. Here's an easy recipe:

Mix together 1½ cups of flour, ½ cup of salt, ½ cup of lukewarm water with food coloring in it, and 1½ tsp. of vegetable oil. Knead until smooth and store in a plastic container.

Worship

Give each teenager a sheet of newsprint and a ball of modeling clay. Using the newsprint as a protective base, have kids each create something with their clay that reflects their personality. For example, someone might create a smiley face to show how he or she loves to laugh. Tell kids that anything goes, as long as their work is original and tasteful.

God's Names

Elohim means omnipotent power and dominion over the whole universe.

El Shaddai refers to God's all-sufficiency and mighty power to accomplish his promises.

Jehovah refers to God's eternal nature.

Jehovah-Rophe means the Lord who heals.

Adonai refers to God's right to possess and rule his creation.

Prince of Peace refers to God's ability to calm our souls, ease our minds, and give us rest.

Jehovah-Rohi refers to God's character as loving, compassionate, and protecting.

(From *Knowing God by His Names* by Dick Purnell, Thomas Nelson Publishers.)

When kids finish, have them take turns explaining their creations to the group. Then ask:

• **Is it fun to use your creativity to make something that represents you? Why or why not?**

• **How are we like clay in God's hands?**

• **Do you think God enjoys creating us to represent him? Why or why not?**

• **How do you think God responds when we complain about how he has created us?**

Read aloud Isaiah 45:9-12. Say: **Every day the thought may cross our minds that if we could just change this part of ourselves or that part of ourselves we would be better. We would be more attractive. We would feel more confident. We would get the cute guy or girl we want.**

Ask:

• **What do you think this passage is saying to us about that attitude? Explain.**

• **Who or what are we worshipping when we have an "I don't accept myself" attitude?**

• **Why do you think this attitude is so offensive to God?**

Say: **When we put ourselves down, in the same breath we are also criticizing God, because we are created in his image. In essence, we're telling God that he messed up, or that he didn't do a good enough job. When we think this way, we are not worshipping him.**

Pause and ask kids how they feel about what you just said. Your kids may have many questions about their struggles with self-acceptance. For example, they may ask, "What if someone is handicapped—how does that reflect God?" or "Is it ever OK to get plastic surgery?" or "What if someone is really overweight—should that person just accept it and move on, or try to change it?" or "Is it wrong to wear makeup?" Allow time to work through these issues with kids. Then say: **We all have weaknesses and imperfections, but God can use those weaknesses to reveal his strength. By accepting ourselves, weaknesses and all, we honor God and welcome him to perfect his strength in us.**

Give each teenager a sheet of paper and a pen and ask kids to write one thing they don't accept about themselves. For example—being an only child, having brown hair, or being too tall (or too short). Then have kids write at least one advantage to that quality. For example, it's better to be short if you want to be a horse jockey or a gymnast. Being an only child may make you more independent or responsible as a result.

When kids are finished, say: **Your parents or lack of parents, your birth order, your family members, and your personal qualities are all a part of what makes you an individual. You can reflect God's image in a way that no one else can—and that makes you special and acceptable.**

Have kids return to their modeling clay and reshape it to represent something they appreciate about God. For example—that he is forgiving, that he is kind, or that he is powerful. When kids are ready, close with a time of open prayer by having kids offer praise prayers to God for what each appreciates most about him.

After the prayer, allow kids to take their sculptures home as a reminder to praise God for creating them in his image.

Hiding From God

Scripture: Hebrews 4:13
Theme: Honesty With God
Experience: In this **prayer of confession**, kids will be reminded that
God sees everything, and encouraged to be totally honest with him.
Preparation: You'll need a Bible, index cards, and pens.

Worship

ive each person an index card and a pen. On their cards, tell kids to write a word or symbol that represents something they've done that they're ashamed of. Tell kids that no one else will see what they write, so they can be totally honest.

When kids finish, have them fold their cards and then form pairs. On "go," have partners go to opposite sides of the room and hide their cards where their partners can't find them. For example, kids might hide their cards under furniture, inside a book, or even somewhere on their bodies. Encourage kids to choose the most secure hiding place they can find. Also, instruct kids not to look at their partners while they're hiding their cards.

Once all the cards are hidden, have pairs rejoin. Have kids scan the other side of the room with their eyes, then try to guess *exactly* where their partners hid their cards. Allow each partner three guesses, making sure kids understand that their guesses must be specific. For example, guessing that the partner's card is "on the other side of the room" is not acceptable. A better guess would be, "Is your card under the left front corner of the piano?" Any guess that isn't exactly right is to be rejected as wrong. After all the kids have guessed, gather everyone together and ask:

- **Did anyone guess correctly?**
- **Why was it so easy for us to hide our "shame" from one another?**
- **Is it also easy to hide our shame from God? Why or why not?**

Read aloud Hebrews 4:13. Then ask:

- **What does this verse say about our ability to hide from God?**
- **Do we still try to hide things from God anyway? Explain.**
- **What are ways we hide from God?**
- **Why is honesty such an important part of worshipping and honoring God?**

Have kids retrieve their cards from their hiding places. Then ask:

- **Can we worship God and be dishonest with him at the same time? Why or why not?**

Say: **Worship and dishonesty don't mix. We all sin every day, and God sees it all. We are being arrogant if we think we can do what we want and get away with it without God knowing. To worship God with a right attitude, we must acknowledge that he knows everything and is everywhere. He can't be fooled. He fills the heaven and the earth. When we sin, we can worship him by honestly confessing what we've done, and genuinely asking his forgiveness.**

Lead the group in a time of confession. Ask kids to think of one thing they're hiding from God. It could be the thing they wrote on their card, or something else. Challenge kids to be honest with God—by silently confessing their secret sins to him, and asking for his forgiveness. As kids confess their sins to God, have them tear up their cards as a way to show that they've received God's forgiveness.

When all (or most) of the cards have been ripped up, close the confessional time with prayer, thanking God for his mercy and forgiveness, and asking him to help kids stay open and honest with him in all things.

Fixing Your Eyes

Scripture: 1 Corinthians 10:31

Theme: Focusing on God

Experience: In this **creative movement** and **sharing time**, teenagers will discover ways to worship God in any circumstance.

Preparation: You'll need a Bible, poster board, tape, and a marker.

Worship

Have a student read aloud 1 Corinthians 10:31. Then ask:

- **What does it mean to "do it all for the glory of God"?**
- **When the passage says, "whatever you do," what kinds of things do you think it's referring to?**
- **Is it possible to give glory to God all the time? Why or why not?**

Say: **Giving glory to God is an attitude of the heart. In this attitude we acknowledge that God is first and the most important person in our lives. It means giving God consistent attention, admiration, and honor.**

Have kids stand up and spin around in circles as fast as they can for fifteen seconds. Kids will be dizzy and unable to walk, so let them sit down and rest until they get their bearings.

Then tell kids they're going to do it again, but this time tell them to find a mark on the wall and stay focused on it as they spin. When they can no longer twist their neck to see the spot, tell them to whip their head around quickly and focus on the spot again. Encourage kids to spin slowly until they understand how to keep their eyes focused on the spot. Then have them go faster.

After fifteen seconds of fast spinning, stop the action. By staying focused, the kids will not get dizzy. Say: **This activity is similar to our spiritual life. If we train ourselves to stay focused on God, then we'll be able to worship him regardless of what we're doing. In essence, we'll get less dizzy in the midst of life's struggles, and we'll honor God by keeping our hearts focused on him. In this way, we can bring glory to God in everything we do. Common actions become holy when they're done with a focus on God.**

Ask kids to brainstorm a list of common actions they do every day, such as eating lunch, talking to Mom, cleaning the kitchen, and so on. Write kids' suggestions on a piece of poster board. Once you've listed around ten items, ask kids to brainstorm ways they can glorify God while doing each of the actions they listed. For example, kids can pray or sing to God while cleaning the kitchen, or they can share their faith with friends while eating lunch at school.

When the list is complete, have kids each choose one act of worship from the list to do every day this week as they go about doing the common things of life. Once kids have chosen their act of worship, have each person offer a one- or two-sentence prayer to God, praising him for who he is and asking him to help the group keep their focus on worshipping him every day.

Unstoppable Praise

Scripture: Psalm 63:1-4

Theme: Spiritual Hunger

Experience: In this **meditation** and **sharing time**, teenagers will experience how it feels to long for God.

Preparation: You'll need Bibles, individual salt packets, water, and cups.

Worship

Once everyone has arrived, ask a volunteer to read aloud Psalm 63:1. Then ask:

• **What do you think it means to "thirst" for God?**

After one or two kids respond, say: **I want to do a little experiment that will help us understand what it means to thirst for God.**

Form pairs. Set out salt packets, water, and cups. Then have each young person swallow part or all of a packet of salt. Don't allow anyone to drink water yet. After everyone has swallowed a packet of salt, ask:

• **How does it feel to be thirsty for water?**

• **What happens to you if you ignore your thirst for too long?**

• **Is it hard to think about anything other than the water? Why or why not?**

Allow everyone to have a cup of water. Once the thirst is washed away, collect the cups and ask:

• **Based on what you've just experienced, what do you think it means to "thirst" for God?**

Say: **When we thirst for God, we think about him all the time. We want him to fill us with his presence, and we don't feel at peace until he does.**

Have someone read aloud Psalm 63:1 again. Then ask:

• **What do you think it means to "long" for God?**

After a few kids respond, say: **Let's do another experiment to see if we can understand what it means to long for God. When I say "go," I want you to hold your breath for at least one minute. I'm going to time you. Ready? Go!**

Not many of the kids will be able to hold their breath for a full minute. That's OK. The goal is to get them to hold their breath for as long as possible.

Once everyone has exhaled, ask:

• **How does it feel for your body to long for air?**

• **What would happen to you if your body couldn't get air?**

• **How is longing for air like longing for God?**

Say: **When you long for God, your heart aches with the desire to be with him. This longing overshadows everything else in life. When you long for God, being in his presence worshipping him is all that matters. Everything else in life seems so much less important compared to worshipping God.**

Ask:

• **Have you felt that kind of longing or thirst for God's presence? Why or why not?**

• **Would you be willing to `ask God to fill you with that longing and thirst for him? Why or why not?**

Read aloud Psalm 63:1-4. Then say: **When David wrote this psalm, he was living in a desert. He knew what it meant to be thirsty. But more than he wanted water, he longed for God's presence. As worshippers, we need to be like that too. We need to be so affected by God's presence that we hunger for it. We have to worship him or it hurts. God wants us to be passionate about our love for him. He wants us to worship him with passion.**

Have kids form a circle, then sit on the floor and face outward. Ask kids to open their Bibles to Psalm 63:1-4. Then say: **If you're willing, God will fill you with a longing to know him and to worship him. I invite you to spend the next few minutes in silence, reading through Psalm 63:1-4, and asking God to make you thirsty so that you long for him just like David did when he lived in the desert.**

Have kids pray silently for up to five minutes. As they finish, give each of them a packet of salt as a reminder to continue asking God to make them thirsty for his presence.

Theme Index

Scripture Index

Old Testament

New Testament

Teaching-Style Index

Act of Commitment

Act of Praise

Group Publishing, Inc.
Attention: Product Development
P.O. Box 481
Loveland, CO 80539
Fax: (970) 679-4370

Evaluation for
Worshipmania

Please help Group Publishing, Inc. continue to provide innovative and useful resources for ministry. Please take a moment to fill out this evaluation and mail or fax it to us. Thanks!

● ● ●

1. As a whole, this book has been (circle one)

not very helpful   very helpful

1   2   3   4   5   6   7   8   9   10

2. The best things about this book:

3. Ways this book could be improved:

4. Things I will change because of this book:

5. Other books I'd like to see Group publish in the future:

6. Would you be interested in field-testing future Group products and giving us your feedback? If so, please fill in the information below:

Name_____

Church Name _____

Denomination _____ Church Size _____

Church Address _____

City _____ State _____ ZIP _____

Church Phone _____

E-mail _____

Exciting Resources for Your Youth Ministry

At Risk: Bringing Hope to Hurting Teenagers

Dr. Scott Larson

Discover how to meet the needs of hurting teenagers with these practical suggestions, honest answers, and tools to help you evaluate your existing programs. Plus, you'll get real-life insights about what it takes to include kids others have left behind. If you believe the Gospel is for everyone, this book is for you! Includes a special introduction by Duffy Robbins and a foreword by Dean Borgman.

ISBN 0-7644-2091-7

All-Star Games From All-Star Youth Leaders

The ultimate game book, from the biggest names in youth ministry! All-time no-fail favorites from Wayne Rice, Les Christie, Rich Mullins, Tiger McLuen, Darrell Pearson, Dave Stone, Bart Campolo, Steve Fitzhugh, and 21 others! You get all the games you'll need for any situation. Plus, you get practical advice about how to design your own games and tricks for turning a *good* game into a *great* game!

ISBN 0-7644-2020-8

The Youth Worker's Encyclopedia of Bible-Teaching Ideas

Here are the most comprehensive idea-books available for youth workers. With more than 365 creative ideas in each of these 400-page encyclopedias, there's at least one idea for every book of the Bible. You'll find ideas for retreats and overnighters...learning games...adventures...projects...affirmations...parties... prayers...music...devotions...skits...and more!

Old Testament	ISBN 1-55945-184-X
New Testament	ISBN 1-55945-183-1

Awesome Worship Services for Youth

These 12 complete worship services involve kids in 4 key elements of worship: celebration, reflection, symbolic action and declaration of God's Truth. Flexible and dynamic services each last about an hour and will bring your group closer to God.

ISBN 0-7644-2057-7

Order today from your local Christian bookstore, or write:
Group Publishing, P.O. Box 485, Loveland, CO 80539.